Governing Science and Technology

PUBLIC ADMINISTRATION AND DEMOCRACY

SERIES EDITOR   DWIGHT WALDO

PUBLISHED

FREDERICK C. MOSHER
Democracy and the Public Service

EMMETTE S. REDFORD
Democracy in the Administrative State

ARTHUR W. MACMAHON
Administering Federalism in a Democracy

OTHER VOLUMES ARE IN PREPARATION

This series originated under the general editorship of the late Roscoe C. Martin.

Governing
Science and Technology

W. HENRY LAMBRIGHT

The Maxwell School, Syracuse University

New York
Oxford University Press
London   1976   Toronto

129758

Dedicated in gratitude
to my mother
and the memory of Roscoe Martin

Preface

In 1970, after three years at the Maxwell School, Syracuse University, teaching courses on the relationship of science and technology to government, I had an opportunity to spend a year as a special assistant in the National Aeronautics and Space Administration (NASA). There, I came to appreciate even more keenly the lack of a book dealing with the administrative politics of large-scale science and technology agencies. I returned to the university with a deep desire to write such a book. At this juncture, I was approached by my friend and colleague, the late Roscoe Martin, who wanted a book focusing on science and technology for his series, "Public Administration and Democracy."

The book I had in mind, we agreed, would fill a critical gap in the literature on this subject. Science and technology writings, insofar as they addressed policy processes at all, generally focused on the role of scientists in decision-making, particularly at the national level. The big agencies and departments, such as NASA, were always mentioned, but more in passing than with direct attention to their policy-making roles. The public administration literature, while more concerned with agencies, tended to be attuned to their operating procedures and research and development (R&D) "management." Students of organization theory approached agencies in more generic fashion, looking for similarities between R&D "organizations" in public and private spheres. Our view was that, while these various streams of intellectual endeavor made significant contributions in their own right, none conveyed the dynamic interaction between science and technology intensive agencies and their political environments. Yet this interaction was a key to understanding the governance of science and technology in the United States. Like the national security and foreign policy arenas, science and technology constituted a particularly "bureaucracy-based" sector of public policy. Options for policy, as well as guidelines for implementation, originated from these agencies. It was important to determine the factors that contributed to policy at the administrative level in order to understand national policy for R&D. The stakes were high. Federal R&D expenditures (now over $20 billion annually) constituted a major national investment. From the evidence available, we believed that administrative agencies and their allies were central actors in determining federal science and technology decisions. By their actions and inactions, they influenced which R&D programs were begun, implemented, or terminated.

This book is an attempt to treat the area we perceived as neglected. It aims not at a major theoretical breakthrough, but at the more modest goal of exploring and analyzing an important, largely uncharted dimension of government in relation to science and technology.

In writing the manuscript, I have had the help of many. First, was Roscoe Martin. Political science and public administration lost one of their very best professionals when he died. Then, there was my colleague, Dwight Waldo, who succeeded Roscoe Martin as editor of the series, and has helped in steering this work to completion. Albert Teich of the Institute for Public Policy Alternatives, State University of New York, also read the entire manuscript and made many telling points that resulted in significant improvements. Indirectly, Francis Rourke of Johns Hopkins and the late Wallace Sayre of Columbia, my first mentors in public administration, contributed to the book. They made clear to me that the important areas of inquiry in the field lay in the intersection, rather than "separation," of politics and bureaucracy.

Political science editors for Oxford University Press, James Amon and Nancy Lane, were very patient during the course of writing. Their suggestions helped to make the book more useful to readers. My superb secretary, Alfreda Lakins, typed and edited many drafts and contributed her own ideas to making this a better book. Finally, thanks are due to Nancy, Dan, and Nat for enduring the preoccupations of a busy husband and father.

To all who helped, I am grateful. Any errors in the book are my responsibility alone.

W.H.L.

Syracuse
March 1975

Foreword

To help us understand the social, economic and political events of our day we use various conceptual frameworks. These conceptual frameworks give us orientation, provide perspective. Thus, for example (among the "larger" ones): competition and conflict between communism and non-communism; "development" of the Third World countries; movement of "advanced" countries from industrialism to post-industrialism. All of such conceptual frameworks have their limitations, but judiciously used they give us understanding of what would otherwise be a chaos of forces and events.

Dialectical interaction between bureaucracy and democracy is surely one of the more useful conceptual frameworks available for understanding the contemporary world. Each of the two, bureaucracy and democracy, is a bundle of artifacts, institutions, sentiments and ideas, given to us by the forces of history and today creating history. Both of the complex of forces had its origins in antiquity, both have played major roles in the development of the modern world. Sometimes they have reinforced each other, sometimes they have come into conflict. Both seem essential to the world we have created and the goals we seek—but there seems to be an area of irreconcilable opposition between them.

The dialectical interaction of bureaucracy and democracy takes place world-wide, in communist as well as non-communist countries, in developing as well as developed countries, and is centrally involved in the transition from industrialism to post-industrialism. Both bureaucracy and democracy are forces within what are ordinarily thought of as private organizations and public organizations; and as the private and public realms (in the movement toward post-industrialism) become more entangled and interactive the appropriate mix of bureaucracy and democracy is the central problem in human values and social mechanics. Nor is it merely a matter of the interaction of bureaucracy and democracy. Over a wide spectrum both bureaucracy and democracy intersect and are intersected by and interact with other familiar concerns and categories: economic productivity, legal interpretation, scientific activity, family affairs, and so forth. In fact, much of the news of any day is a report and commentary on this complex interaction.

The books in this series have as their goal the illumination of various aspects of the interaction of bureaucracy and democracy. In this work Professor Lambright focuses upon the relationship between the scientific and technological enterprises of the United States on the one hand and the United States Government on the other. In that relationship what is, and what should be, the role of administrative institutions, procedures and norms? What is, and what should be, the role of representative institutions, interest groups, public opinion, individual rights—of any forces that may be conceived as democratic? What, indeed, distinguishes bureaucratic and democratic phenomena in actual situations involving the governance of science? What are the dynamics of scientific and technological "advance" and how are they forwarded, or retarded, in what appears to be an inevitable interaction with government? Who makes the important decisions, using what criteria, for whose benefit, with what effects?

It is to such questions that this work is addressed. There are notable works in the area of government and science (those of Don K. Price come first to mind), but altogether it is an inadequately explored area, considering the magnitude of the issues and outcomes involved. This work by Professor Lambright guides us through an area of "administrative politics" about which we must be knowledgeable if we are to successfully mesh our governmental institutions and our scientific and technical enterprises.

DWIGHT WALDO

Contents

Governing Science and Technology

1

Science, Technology, and the Policy Process: An Administrative Perspective

SINCE WORLD WAR II the federal government has become a dominant force behind scientific and technological change in the United States. Private sector organizations perform most of the nation's technical work, but government increasingly provides research and development (R&D) resources and policy direction. Who controls government policy in relation to science and technology? While the answer is far from simple, what is clear is that a major role is played by the operating agencies and departments of the executive branch. They stand at the nexus of government and science and technology. They make the day-to-day decisions, year-in, year-out, that determine who gets what, when, and how in federal research and development. They play a role not only in the execution of policy but also in its formulation.

The science and technology intensive agencies serve to provide a focus for the broader interactions of government, politics, and R&D that are the concern of this book. They constitute a subset of the federal bureaucracy.[1] They link scientists

1. The executive branch may be conceived as having two parts: the Presidency, including the White House Office and the Executive Office of the President, and the bureaucracy, containing the various agencies, departments, commissions, etc. See Richard Schott, *The Bureaucratic State: The Evolution and Scope of the American Federal Bureaucracy* (Morristown, N.J.: General Learning Press, 1974), p. 35.

and technologists to public policy. They are "technocratic" bureaucracies or, as the author calls them, technoscience agencies.[2] These agencies include the Department of Defense (DOD), the National Aeronautics and Space Administration (NASA), the Energy Research and Development Administration (ERDA), the National Science Foundation (NSF), the National Institutes of Health (NIH), and a number of others. Viewed individually and as a group, they are a key locus of science and technology decision-making in the United States. They are among the most important yet least understood or investigated elements in the R&D policy process.

THE PROBLEM

The technoscience agencies are at the heart of the federal R&D function. They represent public administration in its most dramatic role as innovator. The organizations of technoscience have become major agents of change. The amount of money that they control for research, development, and related testing and demonstrations is enormous—over $20 billion in fiscal year 1976.[3] The impact of this money on the people of America and the world, today and tomorrow, is incalculable. These R&D expenditures have significance well beyond their sheer dollar volume. They reach deeply into higher education and the economy. They represent the na-

2. The author is indebted to Dwight Waldo for the term "technoscience." He used the word in an essay, "Reflections on Technoscience Policy and Administration in a Turbulent Milieu." This paper was presented at the Conference on Public Science and Administration at the University of New Mexico, September 1969. The combining of science and technology into technoscience is deliberate. It reflects the fact that these two forces are combined in most federal bureaucracies. Some agencies are more technology-oriented, while some are more science-oriented. Where the distinction needs to be made in this book, it will be made.

3. Because the figure for social sciences is relatively small compared with the whole, research and development (R&D) will be used in this study interchangeably with science and technology. Where a distinction between social sciences and science and technology is important, this will be made. The agencies that are the concern of this book are those that are primarily oriented to natural science and the medical and engineering fields. Those that are social-science related deserve a separate study.

tion's prime investment in its technological future. Technoscience agencies stand where the interests of the President, his
Executive Office, Congress, courts, and other public and private interest groups converge.

Technoscience agencies are where the action is—whether
they wish to be or not. The target of others' claims, they are
themselves major and independent actors in the policy process. Their semi-autonomy within the governmental system derives from a number of factors. The most important is the
Constitution itself. The separation of powers makes Congress
as much a "chief executive" over the technoscience agencies
as the President. Congress not only creates agencies, it sustains
them through authorizations and appropriations. It can make
the lives of their personnel unpleasant and precarious through
the spotlight of investigations. If dissatisfied with a particular
agency's performance, it can destroy that organization. From
the perspective of federal science and technology agencies,
there is not one man on top but many, for Congress consists
of two Houses and many committees and subcommittees. It is
100 Senators, 435 Representatives, and many powerful staffers.
The courts are also an omnipresent force in the life of technoscience agencies. Such agencies can never be quite sure who
their "chief" executive is. Indeed, who that may be at one
point in time may not be at another.

The separation of powers may cause the technoscience
agencies to be uncertain as to their governmental master, but
it also provides options for them. If the Executive is fragmented, policy guidelines from the "leadership" are likely to
be ambiguous at best, inconsistent at worst. The ambiguities
in national science and technology policy will invariably have
to be resolved at the level of the agencies. How a given agency
resolves such matters depends not only on the political pressures of the moment but also on its own sense of institutional
mission.

Every agency has a clientele or, at least, seeks to build one
as protection against Presidential and congressional vicissi-

tudes. Moreover, every agency has organizational identity, usually defined by professional administrative elites that are concerned with the survival and growth of the agency as an institution.[4] Presidents will be in office for eight years at most. The political lifetimes of Congressmen and Senators vary; some of them are longer, some are shorter than those of Presidents. On the other hand, the agencies have missions that extend for decades, even centuries. A consensus forms within the agency as to what its place in national life should be. Over time, an ideology emerges along with standard operating procedures governing administrative behavior in recurring circumstances. There is, thus, an internal logic to technoscience agencies which is independent of immediate environmental forces. The combination of internal and external influences produces an administrative policy. Such a policy may or may not be in accord with national policy as interpreted by a given President.

The technoscience agencies do not escape the charge that is directed at bureaucracy in general: resistance to change. Bureaucratic inertia, however, is not necessarily always evil. Many policies require long-term administrative persistence and commitment. Such qualities must extend over many elections. What a given partisan administration wants may not be in the public interest, as hindsight can easily reveal. The problem derives from the occasion when a mission is completed and an agency substitutes survival for its own sake as a principal goal. There can be serious discontinuities between what the public and its representatives want (policy change) and what a technoscience agency is, in fact, doing (policy maintenance). Change may not always be desirable, but neither is bureaucratic recalcitrance exercised for self-serving ends.

The once popular notions, that there is a politics/administration dichotomy and that politicians make policy and ad-

4. See Philip Selznick, *Leadership in Administration* (New York: Harper & Row, 1957).

ministrators carry it out, have been abandoned by most theorists. But the *issue* of the appropriate role of administration in politics/policy has not been resolved. Administrators and their agencies do engage in politics in the sense of influencing "authoritative allocations of values."[5] The technoscience agencies influence policy formation as well as policy implementation. But how? With what consequences? To the extent that an administrative politics/policy exists, what is its relationship to national policy/politics?

The technoscience agencies are the cutting edge of federal bureaucracy. They are at bureaucracy's forefront in terms of the *substance* of work—R&D. They bring R&D to bear on their mission responsibilities; for a few, R&D is their mission, at least as they define it. They are also at the forefront of bureaucracy in respect to *organization* of work, particularly in the use of grants and contracts to outside, largely private-sector institutions. The problems of technoscience agencies epitomize governmental dilemmas that increasingly confront democracy and public administration.

By understanding the dynamics of a discrete set of agencies engaged in the politics and administration of a particular policy function, greater light may be shed on the interaction of bureaucracy and national policy in general. The fact of bureaucracy's politics/policy role creates a critical issue in democracy. The bureaucracy is not elected. It is, in theory, an instrument of democracy: a tool. Who controls this tool? To whom or to what is bureaucracy responsible? These are the key questions in the relationship of public administration to democracy, particularly when agencies most directly and deeply concerned with science and technology are at issue.

THE APPROACH

A major difficulty in addressing the subject at hand in any systematic way stems from the fragmentation of "the" science

5. David Easton, *A Framework for Political Analysis* (Englewood Cliffs, N.J.: Prentice-Hall, 1965), p. 50.

and technology function. Compare technoscience agencies and R&D policy with some analogous bureaucracy/policy combinations: the Department of Defense in military policy; the State Department in foreign policy; the Department of Agriculture in agricultural policy; and so forth. In contrast to these relatively sharply defined relationships, science and technology agencies and policies are seemingly everywhere—and nowhere. In getting a better grasp on the problem, the concept of "policy space," as developed by Anthony Downs, is helpful. Downs has shown that there are a variety of policy spaces, or governmental functions, to which different agencies may relate to one degree or another. He notes that "a given space can be occupied by several bureaus simultaneously if they all have functions involving that space."[6] Thus, many agencies are in the "policy space" of R&D, but some more so than others. There are certain agencies that are primarily concerned with the science and technology function, such as the National Science Foundation, the National Aeronautics and Space Administration, and the Energy Research and Development Administration. The Department of Defense regards science and technology as a sub-mission of its operational military objectives, but it considers R&D as an exceptionally important sub-mission. Indeed, DOD occupies a major portion of science and technology "territory." With FY-1976 expenditures estimated at $9.9 billion, DOD is the largest science and technology spender of all.[7] For many other agencies, however, science and technology are much lower in priority. To the extent that an agency spends some money on R&D, it may lay claim to being a technoscience agency and to occupying at least a marginal role in the policy space of science and technology. While all agencies are not equal in relationship to

6. Anthony Downs, *Inside Bureaucracy* (Boston, Mass.: Little, Brown, 1967), p. 212.

7. The role of DOD illustrates the fact that a single agency or department can have locations in a variety of policy spaces. It may largely control one and be just another actor in others. See Downs, *op. cit.,* chap. 17 for an elaboration of the policy space concept, particularly as it relates to bureau territoriality.

R&D, even the lesser actors have significance. The Department of Housing and Urban Development and the Department of Transportation, for example, are important in the application of new technology to many domestic problems under their purview. By including them as technoscience agencies, however, the difficulty in charting the administrative boundaries of R&D policy is increased. The complexity cannot be avoided. There is simply no one dominant center of decision-making in science and technology policy in the federal government. The "agency-spread" is wide. The policy is diffuse. How is such a disparate set of organizations, such an amorphous policy arena, to be approached, much less understood?

Don K. Price, a pioneer in government and R&D studies, found it helpful to consider policy-making in this area to flow from the interaction of various "estates." These estates differ from one another in their training and skills.[8]

First, there is the *scientific estate*. This is concerned solely with truth for its own sake. "For a basic approach of modern science has been to purge itself of a concern for purposes and values," said Price, "in order to deal more reliably with the study of material phenomena and their causes and effects."[9] Second, comes the *professional estate*. "The professions (for example, engineering and medicine) make tremendous use of the findings of the sciences, but they add something more: a purpose. Science has advanced by getting rid of the idea of purpose, except the abstract purpose of advancing truth and knowledge. But the profession puts it back again. . . ."[10]

Third, is the *administrative estate*. "The general administrator is," said Price, ". . . not a professional: his responsibility is not restricted to some special aspect of an organization's affairs that is related to a special body of knowledge or a special type of training, and it is more difficult for him to

8. Don K. Price, *The Scientific Estate* (Cambridge: Harvard University Press, 1965), p. 135.
9. *Ibid.*, p. 122.
10. *Ibid.*, p. 133.

define a sense of obligation to a professional purpose that to some degree transcends the purposes of his employer. . . . he must be prepared to understand and to use a wide variety of professional expertise and scholarly disciplines, as he helps his political superior (or the directors of a business corporation) attain their general purposes."[11]

Finally, there is the *political estate.* "Still further away from the precision and abstraction of the sciences and from the self-discipline and body of established principles of the true profession, are the politicians. The men who exercise legislative or executive power may make use of the skills of administrators and engineers and scientists, but in the end they make their most important decisions on the basis of value judgments or hunch or compromise or power interests. . . . In government, the politician is apt to make every decision both to accomplish its ostensible purpose and to maintain or increase his power—just as in private business, the principal executive or owner is apt to make every decision, both to produce some product or service and to make a profit."[12]

Price made it clear that the various estates could not be "sharply distinguished" but "fall along a gradation or spectrum within our political system. At one end of the spectrum, pure science is concerned with knowledge and truth; at the other end, pure politics is concerned with power and action." While constituting ideal types seldom existing in pure form, these estates affected behavior of men and institutions. As Price declared:

. . . men and institutions tend to associate themselves with one function or another, and many of the more interesting problems of politics arise from the ways in which these four types cooperate or conflict with one another. Their relationships have not made obsolete the classic concern of political science with the relations among branches or levels of government, and between them and competing political parties and economic or ideological interests.

11. *Ibid.,* pp. 133–34.
12. *Ibid.,* p. 134.

But they have added a significant and interesting complication to the study of contemporary politics, and one that will be of growing importance as long as science continues to increase its influence on public affairs.[13]

In focusing as he does on the interaction of groups with particular biases and ideologies based on their training and experience, Price follows a tradition in political analysis pioneered by Harold Lasswell. Lasswell, years before, had posited the existence of a "skill commonwealth" and had argued that groups could gain influence, not on the basis of geography or class, but through their exercise of a common set of skills that could be taught and learned.[14]

The Price concepts are suggestive. "Estates analysis" would appear to be another form of interest group analysis. What the estates approach highlights, however, is that, for some groups, interest and even power within government are related to their special skills. A *function* of government is, by definition, a "special" part of government. Those concerned with it will be groups with interests that are function-specific. In science and technology policy, the scientific and technological estates will surely be involved because of their skills. As in all areas of government, there will be bureaucrats and politicians. Emmette S. Redford points out that, while the Price estates may be relevant as guides to actors in decision-making *within* government, there are many actors *outside* government (not included in the four estates) who also can affect policy. Specifically, Redford adds: ". . . power brokers outside government, the opinion makers, and the strictly lay participants in policy-making centers." "Indeed," says Redford, "outside all these groups of participants is the eighth

13. *Ibid.,* p. 135.
14. Harold D. Lasswell, *The Analysis of Political Behaviour: An Empirical Approach* (New York: Oxford University Press, 1948), p. 134; Robert C. Wood, "The Rise of an Apolitical Elite," *Scientists and National Policy Making,* Robert Gilpin and Christopher Wright, eds. (New York and London: Columbia University Press, 1964), p. 46; Heinz Eulau, "Skill Revolution and Consultative Commonwealth," *American Political Science Review,* Vol. 67, March 1973, pp. 169–91.

estate—all of us who are not regular participants in most are-nas of decision making."[15]

Although many estates may be active, there is little question that scientists and engineers will have some degree of influ-ence in the R&D policy arena *because* of their skills. The na-ture of R&D decision-making involves technical judgments as to: "Can it be done?" Answers to that question require the expertise of technically trained people. How *much* influence the technical estates have is another matter. The other ques-tion always at issue is: "Should it be done?" Here is where estates other than scientists and engineers may hold sway. In discussing this latter question, the scientific estate, for exam-ple, cannot perform as it would in labs, but more as an advo-cate for particular policy positions. Even where purely tech-nical judgments are made, human factors of personality and values may enter into the premises of scientific and techno-logical calculations.[16] In short, while identifying relevant ac-tors in science and technology policy, the Price scheme may indicate more how given estates are supposed to behave than how they, in fact, do act.

The division of estates is not at all clear. Many adminis-trators in technoscience agencies are also technocrats. That is, they have technical backgrounds. Do they play Price's admin-istrative role, or do they mirror their professional biases? Frederick Mosher argues that agencies and departments are dominated largely by career bureaucrats, but these bureau-crats relate primarily to particular *professions* associated with the function they perform. "For better or worse—or better *and* worse—much of our government is now in the hands of professionals (including scientists)," states Mosher.[17] He sees

15. Emmette S. Redford, *Democracy in the Administrative State* (New York: Oxford University Press, 1969), p. 69.

16. For a study of scientists in political roles, see Robert Gilpin, *American Scientists and Nuclear Weapons Policy* (Princeton, N.J.: Princeton University Press, 1962).

17. Frederick C. Mosher, *Democracy and the Public Service* (New York: Oxford University Press, 1968), p. 132.

government policy as the resultant of many forces, but he points out that the bureaucracy is increasingly playing a major policy role. To the extent that the administrators identify with professions, he is suggesting that the modern state is becoming an instrument of the professionals. This would imply that the answer to the question of who governs technoscience agencies is: the technocrats.

One does not have to agree with Mosher to recognize the importance of his point. Should an agency be captured by any one estate (be it scientific, professional, administrative, or political), there are serious implications for agency and national policy. Ordinarily, agency decisions reflect group processes (i.e., the inputs of many estates). As J. K. Galbraith has written, large organizations, public and private, are increasingly run by a broad collective entity that he calls the "technostructure."[18] The technostructure reflects the growing involvement of technical specialists in decision-making; it "embraces all who bring specialized knowledge, talent, or experience to group decision-making. This, not the management, is the guiding intelligence—the brain—of the enterprise."[19] Some groups, or estates, may be more important in certain organizations than others, skewing the decisions of the technostructure one way or another. In focusing on technoscience agencies, the role of the various estates in agency decision-making will therefore be a key issue for attention.

"Estates analysis" thus can help in explaining policy formation; so, also, can "organizational analysis."[20] In the latter, the agency-as-a-whole is viewed as an interest group. There are basic organizational stakes in survival that go beyond the claims of any single estate. How agencies gauge their interests

18. John Kenneth Galbraith, *The New Industrial State* (Boston, Mass.: Houghton Mifflin, 1967), p. 71.

19. *Ibid.*

20. The distinction is akin to the two paradigms used by Graham Allison: bureaucratic politics and organization process. These appear in his "Conceptual Models and the Cuban Missile Crisis," *The American Political Science Review*, Vol. 63, September 1969, pp. 689–718.

and what this implies for policy, depends on the interaction of agencies with their political environments. Agencies must relate both to an environment of subsystem politics and one of macropolitics.

Subsystem politics is "normal" politics for the technoscience agencies. As defined by Redford, it is the politics of function, where the central actors are an agency, its congressional committees, and those external interest groups most concerned with what the agency does or does not do.[21] Since other subsystem actors often have a perspective identical to the agency—promoting the given function with which they are all concerned—there is a general problem that subsystem politics and administrative policy will diverge from macropolitics[22] and national policy. The agency is "closest" to subsystem politics. The pressures at the subsystem level are immediate and direct. Those at the macro-level tend to be distant, both in a psychological and temporal sense. Hence, agency/subsystem policy may stay the same while national policy shifts.

How are these two levels of policy and politics then brought into closer coherence? Which governs the other? Perhaps the incongruity will create conflict situations. When subsystem politics fail to represent new value-orientations, an issue may rise to the highest level, involving the President and Congress-as-a-whole for final determination. At this level, a larger number and a different set of interests become involved in a given policy sector.

The following chapters will be guided by an approach that emphasizes estates and agencies as political interest groups. The purpose of the book is to use political and administrative

21. Redford, *op. cit.*, pp. 96–102. For a pioneering attempt to understand politics at the subsystem level, see J. Leiper Freeman, *The Political Process: Executive Bureau—Legislative Committee Relations* (New York: Random House, 1955).
22. Redford, *op. cit.*, p. 107. Macropolitics was defined by Redford "as the politics that arises when the community-at-large and the leaders of government-as-a-whole are brought into the discussion and determination of issues."

analysis of the "middle range" better to understand the dynamics of federal decision-making in science and technology. It is obvious that much of the force of policy is centered at the administrative level of governance. This being the case, it is crucial to grasp the interaction of administrative agencies, science and technology, and national policy. The problem is to comprehend how specialized functional policy is formed and how it is integrated (or not integrated) into a more general, national policy. Succeeding chapters examine the process by which science and technology programs are established, implemented, terminated, and changed. They look at research, development, and the interface between R&D and operations. They focus on the role of technoscience agencies in each of these phases of the R&D process. Before studying the pieces of the R&D picture, it is necessary first to provide an overview of the recent evolution of relations between government and science and technology.

THE BACKGROUND

There have been six distinct periods in the interaction of science, technology, and government since 1940. The first was the wartime era, 1940–45; the second embraced the postwar years, 1945–50; the third extended from 1950 to the launching of Sputnik in 1957; the fourth lasted a decade, from 1957 to 1967, when a combination of war in Vietnam and social problems at home ended the accelerated growth of R&D expenditures. From 1967 to 1971 there was a fifth period of government/science and technology interaction. During this time federal funding for R&D fell. Since 1971 expenditures have begun rising again, dramatically, in selected fields such as cancer research and energy research.

1940–45. During the war the basic outlines of the modern government/science and technology relationship were drawn. What was important was not only the enormous increase in money to R&D, but the way the funds were managed. As Don Price has stated, ". . . the most significant discovery or devel-

opment . . . was not the technical secrets that were involved
in radar or the atomic bomb; it was the administrative system
and set of operating policies that produced such technological
feats."[23]

Under the National Defense Research Committee set up in
1940 and the Office of Scientific Research and Development
(OSRD) established in 1941, the nation's scientific and technological resources were mobilized. While many scientists
and engineers came directly into government service, most
others performed their work for the defense effort under contract where they were, in university and industrial labs.
OSRD was placed in the Executive Office of the President,
and its head, Vannevar Bush, constituted President Franklin
Roosevelt's unofficial science adviser. OSRD served as a clear-
inghouse for much of the wartime R&D intended for the
Army, Navy, National Advisory Committee for Aeronautics,
and other agencies. OSRD could also initiate whatever R&D
projects it deemed promising. The most dramatic of OSRD's
projects was to build an atomic bomb. OSRD began the
atomic energy program, transferred it to the Army in 1943
only after much of the R&D had been done, and retained substantial connection thereafter.[24] While most of the development work was accomplished by the operating agencies and
departments of the bureaucracy and, through them, by the
universities and industry, OSRD maintained strong control
over the entire wartime enterprise. The location of OSRD
within the Executive Office of the President and in the Office
for Emergency Management (OEM) was crucial to its power,
especially when combined with the wartime atmosphere that
created a mood of cooperation from all parts of the R&D system in the pursuit of victory and removed all normal restric-

23. Cited in U.S. Congress, House Committee on Science and Astronautics,
Subcommittee on Science, Research and Development, Report: *Toward a
Science Policy for the United States* (Washington, D.C.: USGPO, 1970), p. 81.
Hereinafter cited as *Toward a Science Policy* (1970).
24. J. Stefan Dupré and Sanford A. Lakoff, *Science and the Nation* (Engle-
wood Cliffs, N.J.: Prentice-Hall, 1962), p. 10.

tions based on funding or congressional oversight. As Price pointed out:

> As the head of an independent agency in the OEM, Vannevar Bush had every right to go directly to the President on issues involving the use of science and scientists during World War II. A position of direct responsibility to the President was not important mainly in order to let Dr. Bush as head of OSRD have personal conversations with President Roosevelt. It was much more important to give him the leverage he needed in dealing with the vast network of administrative relationships on which the success of a Government agency depends. This is the point that is completely missed by those who think that the ideal position for a scientific agency in Government is one of complete separation from the political executive.[25]

1945–50. In 1939 federal science and technology expenditures stood at $50 million. Most of the money was spent by the Department of Agriculture. The bulk of federal R&D was performed in the government's own laboratories.[26] At the close of the war, in 1945, the government was spending $1.5 billion, primarily for defense and mainly via contracts to private organizations.[27] The war had brought vast, unprecedented change to federal administration. The R&D function had come into its own. From 1945 to 1950 this administrative revolution was consolidated. Centralized wartime controls on government R&D were relaxed in the immediate postwar years, as OSRD phased out. In fact, the decentralized pattern for governing federal science and technology that was adopted, *de facto,* between 1945 and 1950, was at the opposite pole from the wartime experience.

Science and technology were now an important segment of government, part of the missions of various operating agencies and departments. This bureaucracy had become "techno-

25. Don K. Price, *Government and Science* (New York: New York University Press, 1954). Cited in *Toward a Science Policy* (1970), p. 80.
26. Dupré and Lakoff, *op. cit.,* p. 9.
27. The budget figure is reported in *Toward a Science Policy* (1970), p. 115.

cratic," and it wanted no part of a civilian OSRD. Nor did the scientists and engineers who had pioneered the new government and R&D relationship. They feared centralized power almost as much as did the new technoscience agencies. The closest proposal to a civilian OSRD was that of Bush in his 1945 report to the President, *Science, The Endless Frontier*.[28] Bush proposed what became the National Science Foundation. It would be the lead agency within the bureaucracy for sponsoring basic scientific research. In the five years that it took to get NSF established, however, the military agencies, AEC, and NIH moved into the vacuum left by OSRD. The wartime pattern of government-by-contract was continued. There was increasing use of grants to universities for basic research in accord with the preferences of the scientific community. During the war the federal relationship was almost exclusively with technology and applied research. In the postwar period basic research began to be supported by government to a degree that the scientific community could hardly have imagined prior to 1940.

1950–57. The 1945–50 period was one in which a growing federal responsibility for R&D became increasingly accepted as "normal." Also part of peacetime "normalcy" was the cold war between the United States and the Soviet Union. During 1950–57 the interests of science and technology and national security were joined. While expenditures for health-related research grew, the dominant spending technoscience agencies were military or military-related, such as the AEC. The application of science and technology to economic growth and the general welfare was secondary in priority. The Korean conflict, the explosion of the Soviet hydrogen bomb—these events combined to cast a long military shadow over all R&D expenditures. The nation's scientists and universities found that they could even satisfy much of their own needs for basic research in the name of defense. Some of the least restrictive

28. Vannevar Bush, *Science, The Endless Frontier* (Washington, D.C.: USGPO, reprint 1960).

administrative procedures for basic research within the executive branch were those of the military agencies. As expenditures for R&D continued to grow, the Bureau of the Budget occasionally called on NSF to exercise more national policy leadership—a task for which it had legislative authority. But NSF had neither the bureaucratic power nor the inclination to fulfill this role. Federal science and technology obligations reached $4.4 billion in 1957. They continued to be administered in an extremely decentralized manner.

1957–67. Then came the technological surprise of Sputnik. For a decade, the U.S. policy for R&D was clear: pre-eminence —to be first in all scientific and technological fields, but particularly in those related to defense and national prestige. That was *de facto* national science and technology policy. For several years after 1957, annual federal R&D funding increased at an accelerated pace. Basic research rose at an average of 15 percent per year. By 1967, federal R&D obligations had reached $17.1 billion. A major reason for the increase lay in the creation of the National Aeronautics and Space Administration (NASA) in 1958 and the decision by President John F. Kennedy in 1961 that the United States, through NASA, should "commit itself to achieving the goal, before this decade is out, of landing a man on the moon and returning him safely to earth."[29]

NASA epitomized the drive by the United States for "pre-eminence." It added that special bit of adventure and glamor to what many scientists later called their "Golden Years." The Defense Department, however, continued to be by far the most significant spender in federal R&D. Indeed, when President Dwight Eisenhower created a White House science policy advisory apparatus in 1957, led by an Office of Special Assistant to the President for Science and Technology and the President's Science Advisory Committee (PSAC), he did so in part to get help in making choices among the many weapons proposals being pushed on him from the Pentagon.

29. *Toward a Science Policy* (1970), p. 100.

The White House science and technology policy apparatus was further strengthened in 1962 when an Office of Science and Technology (OST) was established.

A Sputnik-induced innovation at the subcabinet level was the Federal Council for Science and Technology (FCST) which was activated in 1959 and, like the Executive Office bodies, was headed by the President's science adviser. FCST's birth reflected and encouraged the elevation of scientists and engineers in the executive branch. A number of assistant departmental secretaries with responsibilities for R&D were appointed. The Pentagon led the way in reforms at the administrative level with the establishment of an Advanced Research Projects Agency (ARPA) in 1958. It was independent of the services and responsible to a new top-level Pentagon official: the Director of Defense Research and Engineering (DDR&E). This individual not only served as science adviser to the Secretary of Defense but also had authority for managing all defense R&D.

Science and technology were thus strengthened throughout the executive branch, and congressional interest in science and technology grew, as well. The basic pattern of decentralized, pluralistic governance remained intact, however. NSF's national policy responsibilities were transferred to OST. While OST may have tried to bring more centralized direction to the nation's R&D establishment, it found itself too small, too weak, and too busy a staff organization. As a congressional report later noted, "In essence, its work has been more akin to fire fighting than fire prevention."[30]

More importantly, there was not the impetus from the President during this period for central control of federal science and technology. On the contrary, Lee Dubridge, President Nixon's first science adviser, told Congress:

When research and development were growing at such a rapid rate, and extending into so many fields of science and technology,

30. *Ibid.*, p. 94.

and, when there was strong public support for this rapid growth, the need for a Federal policy governing Federal research and development did not seem urgent. As a matter of fact, there was some fear that the adoption of a specific policy statement might be more restrictive than encouraging to federal R&D activities. Such policy as existed, mostly in unwritten form, encouraged each agency of the government to pursue and support such R&D activities as it deemed necessary and desirable, applying such a fraction of its overall budgetary allocations to R&D as the agency deemed to be a good investment.[31]

Thus, for a decade, there was constant growth in federal R&D. Funds for basic research and universities were plentiful, and government stimulated and paid for the training of thousands of new scientists and engineers. With the coming of Lyndon Johnson's "Great Society" in the mid-1960's, there were new departments (the Department of Housing and Urban Development and the Department of Transportation) funding science and technology. Then the Golden Years of R&D ended.

1967–71.   There was no one event to compare with Sputnik that dramatically signaled the end of the former period and the beginning of this one. R&D could not grow forever at the post-Sputnik pace. On the other hand, the suddenness of the cessation came as a shock, both to technoscience agencies and their clients. What ended the rise so abruptly was the combination of Vietnam and the domestic crises in the cities. Neither priority was R&D intensive. For the most part the war used existing technology rather than developing new technology. At the same time science and technology were not as central to the problems of cities as they were to the space program. The inflation that accompanied war against "communism" in Southeast Asia and against poverty at home ate deeply into R&D. As the rise of NASA had heralded the Golden Years, so its decline stood as a symbol of change. In 1969 NASA achieved its goal of a lunar landing. Within a few

31. *Ibid.,* p. 91.

years its budget was only half what it had been at its mid-1960's peak. There were some areas of growth in housing, transportation, and other domestic/social fields, but these were very small gains when measured against declines in the big technology agencies. Thus, in 1968 federal obligations for R&D *fell* to $16.5 billion. In 1969 they declined further to $15.6 billion. In 1970 they dropped again to $15.3 billion. In this period of decline as well as of rising inflation, scientists and engineers suddenly found themselves out of work or underworked. Many questioned their "relevance."

This period was not just one of budgetary exigency; it was also one of shifting public attitudes toward technology and even science. These attitudes were very general but inevitably touched on federal R&D. In part, they were simply anti-technological. There was the feeling that technology had gotten out of democratic control.[32] In addition, the attitudes were anti-military. The Vietnam conflict revealed for critics of the war what they saw as the "subverting" of science and technology and their institutions, including the university, to destructive purposes.[33] Moreover, the new mood arose from a positive interest in environmental issues; uncontrolled science and technology, it was felt, were despoiling and polluting the earth. In 1969 the National Environmental Policy Act (NEPA) was passed and as a result, in 1970, a new Council on Environmental Quality (CEQ) and the Environmental Protection Agency (EPA) came into being. In requiring the filing of environmental impact statements, NEPA indicated that government technology would be subjected to scrutiny for its environmental costs as well as economic benefits.

Finally, the new climate of opinion related to the fall of the

32. The flavor of this mood can be seen in the writings of Herbert Marcuse, *One-Dimensional Man* (Boston: Beacon Press, 1964); and Jacques Ellul, *The Technological Society* (New York: Alfred A. Knopf, 1964). Such literature gained general widespread attention during this period. See also chap. 2, "Philosophers of the Technological Age," in Albert H. Teich, ed., *Technology and Man's Future* (New York: St. Martin's Press, 1972).

33. See Dorothy Nelkin, *The University and Military Research* (Ithaca, N.Y.: Cornell University Press, 1972).

university, the institution of science, from public and governmental favor. Universities seemed unable to provide solutions to difficult social problems facing the country. Ironically, while universities were chastised for irrelevance by some, they were pilloried by others for being too relevant to the Pentagon. For many, however, the universities lost credibility because their handling of student riots and uprisings during this time suggested that they were incapable of managing themselves, much less helping the country deal with its problems. The nation began expecting less of universities. It demanded less of science. In dollars that took account of inflation, federal funding for academic research consequently fell 17 percent between 1967 and 1971.[34] In every sense this was a period of economic recession for R&D. It was one of transition in public/governmental attitudes toward science and technology. It left many scientists, engineers, industry and university executives, and even government officials bewildered and embittered.

Since 1971. In 1971 the federal science and technology budget began a "recovery." Obligations stood at $15.5 billion in FY–1971; $16.5 billion in FY–1972; $16.8 billion in FY–1973; $17.4 billion in FY–1974; about $18.7 billion in FY–1975; and an estimated $21.6 billion in FY–1976. Nearly half of federal R&D went to the Defense Department, whose R&D spending gained considerably once the United States military involvement in Vietnam ended. However, as a percentage of overall R&D spending, Defense was actually falling because other sectors were on the rise.

This was not to say that the technoscience agencies and associated clientele were prospering again. With inflation rates reaching double digits in this period, the level of support for most programs was still not what it was in 1967 in terms of non-inflated dollars. But the trend, at least, was upward, and this buoyed some technocratic spirits. Furthermore, *certain*

34. Harvey Brooks, "Are Scientists Obsolete?" *Science*, Vol. 186, November 8, 1974, p. 501.

fields were experiencing dramatic upswings. Apollo-style rhetoric was used in 1971 when President Nixon launched a crusade against cancer. Similar language was applied when Project Independence—an effort to make America self-sufficient in energy—came into being during the Arab oil embargo of 1973–74. From the energy crisis emerged a major reorganization of federal technoscience. In late 1974, legislation was passed that created a major new agency on the federal R&D scene: the Energy Research and Development Administration. ERDA subsumed the Atomic Energy Commission (AEC) and smaller energy R&D units located in other agencies. The regulatory side of AEC was split off and placed in a new Nuclear Regulatory Commission (NRC).

The science and technology agencies were regaining their strength at the very time the capacity of the President to govern this segment of bureaucracy seemed to be weakening. In 1973 President Nixon demolished the entire White House science policy advisory apparatus and divided this advisory function between the director of NSF (for civil R&D) and the National Security Council (for military R&D). Leaders of the scientific community lobbied hard to reverse what they regarded both as a demotion for science and the creation of a dangerous vacuum in technical inputs to Presidential decision-making. In May 1975 it appeared they might succeed when President Ford "pledged . . . to key members of Congress that he would act to re-establish as a permanent part of the White House organization, the Office of Science and Technology that his predecessor abolished."[35]

Meanwhile, Congress was attempting to assert a new role in technoscience. In 1972 it created the Office of Technology Assessment (OTA) to provide greater legislative leverage over the executive branch in science and technology affairs. Relating to Congress in much the same way as the General Ac-

35. "Ford to Seek Re-Establishment of White House Science Office," *New York Times*, May 23, 1975.

counting Office, OTA could be useful to Congress in over-seeing technology and helping to push technoscience agencies to consider the broader implications of their R&D programs early in the decision-making process.

Moreover, in 1974, as a result of the passage of the Congressional Budget and Impoundment Control Act, the Congressional Budget Office (CBO) was established, with a new Budget Committee in both the House and Senate to "write resolutions laying out total spending, spending priorities, total revenue and the appropriate budget surplus or deficit for the coming fiscal year." The full Senate and House, "which never before have come to grips with these broad budget concepts," were "to agree on a budget resolution. . . ." Thus, "Budget Committee members are in a position to have great influence over the pattern of federal spending."[36] Much depends upon when and how such tools as OTA and CBO are used. A major problem in overall congressional power to assess technology or influence "the" executive budget lies in the lack of control by Congress-as-a-whole over the various congressional committees. Such functional committees have interests similar to those of the agencies in resisting comprehensive efforts in public management, whether by the President or Congress.

The congressional initiatives were part of a general "management" thrust evolving in this period that had significant implications for technoscience. The anti-technology mood had dissipated somewhat. The nation seemed committed, or at least reconciled, to maintaining and strengthening the R&D function—but more on the terms of government than those of scientific and engineering researchers. One dimension of the management trend lay in a stronger effort to set priorities and to maintain economy and efficiency in R&D. The effort to "target" basic research in cancer studies was symptomatic of this trend. At the same time, there was a new cognizance that

36. Joel Havemann, "Congress Report/New Budget Committees Already Have Ambitious Plans," *National Journal*, September 28, 1974, p. 1445.

science and technology could create problems as well as solve them. In this sense, management of technology related to a new quest for anticipatory policy.

There was an ambivalence in the government's overall relationship to science and technology. Various government agencies sought to stimulate the technological genie, while others sought just as strongly to put it back in the bottle. Thus, the military developed more sophisticated weapons, while the State Department and Arms Control and Disarmament Agency (ACDA) worked equally assiduously to limit their use through international agreements. Similarly, for virtually every energy solution put forth by the new energy agency, the Environmental Protection Agency would be on guard for possible environmental dangers. Such bureaucratic conflict seemed far afield from rationalistic "management" notions being emphasized at the same time. But neither bureaucratic politics nor management techniques would likely lead to a national policy for science and technology—at least, one set independently of technoscience agencies and their allies.

2

Launching Technology

THE SUPERSONIC TRANSPORT, Apollo, Space Shuttle, B1 Bomber, Trident Submarine, and Liquid Metal Fast Breeder Reactor—such large-scale programs as these stand at the forefront of federal R&D policy. They are the most visible and controversial part of federal science and technology expenditures. The stakes for all parties concerned with these programs are immense. Billions of dollars are often involved, along with hundreds of thousands of skilled technical and managerial professionals. A decade or more may pass between the time a program is initiated and the time it is completed. The $24 billion Apollo project represents the quintessence of the large-scale technological program. It and other big technology efforts serve to make more visible the political dynamics that are present in many lesser, but still important, development efforts.

Development, the second half and far more expensive side of R&D, can be defined as follows:

. . . the design, fabrication, testing and evaluation of full-scale prototypes of materials, devices, systems, or processes. These can be very complex devices such as missiles, aircraft, space vehicles, and nuclear reactors. They can be entire "systems" such as those for air defense or for air traffic control. For testing and evaluation, many prototypes may be ordered, and the expenses of tests are those under actual "field" conditions.[1]

Federal technology development programs constitute a fulcrum for federal R&D policy. They affect not only applied research, but also basic research expenditures in the agencies sponsoring development. Basic research is influenced to the extent that the scientific disciplines that are given priority by technoscience agencies are those relevant to development goals. Since technology is not usually applied until it is technically "ripe" for exploitation, development stands not at the end but at a strategic middle in the R&D sequence—between basic research and applications. Development programs are efforts to create specific new technologies. How are such programs born? How are they "sold" throughout the political process? How are they maintained?

Milton Shaw, who was at one time responsible for the Liquid Metal Fast Breeder Reactor, the nation's highest priority energy R&D program, has stated: "Bringing to completion long-term technology projects is one of the toughest problems that a democratic society faces." "The political process," Shaw continues, "inevitably focuses attention on short-term payoff, and long-range programs, whatever their promise, have a difficult time surviving."[2] Claude Barfield, former science policy reporter for the *National Journal,* notes that large-scale development programs must "take their chances with changes in Presidential administrations, fluctuations in the national economy, variations in fiscal restraints—both governmentwide and for their managing agencies—and, finally, changes in the requirements of the missions for which they were intended."[3]

1. U.S. Congress, House Committee on Government Operations, 34th Report, *Federal Research and Development Programs: The Decision-Making Process* (Washington, D.C.: USGPO, 1966), p. 6.
2. Claude E. Barfield, "Energy Report/U.S. Retains Commitment to Breeder Reactor Despite Environmental, Economic Challenges," *National Journal,* December 15, 1973, p. 1865.
3. Claude E. Barfield, "Space Report/Fund Cutback for Nuclear Rocket

There is no question that the big development programs have numerous hurdles to overcome in order to survive. Yet there are many critics of these programs who can point to examples of efforts that they feel survived far too long. They see various technology programs as having a momentum of their own. Once established, they become extremely difficult to terminate (according to these critics). For them, the breeder project Shaw once headed is a very dangerous program, given its environmental hazards. They see the problem for democracy not as keeping such programs going but of shutting them off or even preventing their birth altogether. They cite SST as an example not of how difficult it is to complete a program, but of how long a program can be kept alive in spite of its numerous failings.

Such varying points of view suggest that technology programs are never far from the controversial issues of the day. Their tangible "hardware" character may, in fact, make them excellent targets for enemies, as well as rallying points for defenders of particular causes. When a debate over a development project becomes macropolitical, that fact may be due to what the technology symbolizes to numerous parties to an existing conflict. The stakes of contestants may be economic, bureaucratic, or ideological. The technology provides an opportunity for the focusing of attention. The politics of science seldom rise beyond the subsystem level of participation. Technology much more frequently escalates to macropolitics. It may be very difficult, for example, to mobilize support or opposition to defense spending in general, but a specific weapons project can place in sharp relief an otherwise ambiguous subject.

The technoscience agencies stand at the center of any debate over large-scale development programs. A given agency is a sponsor, manager, host, and defender of its technology efforts. Unless it is vigilant, it may also become captive to its

Engine Worries Space Backers in Congress," *National Journal*, May 29, 1971. See "Nerva Development," p. 1160.

own programs. Just as agencies represent a problem in control
for government and democracy generally, the large-scale technology programs within agencies become powerful forces in
their own right. They can build up impetus and constituency
independent of their administrative home.

The stakes, positive and negative, are great for the agency
that is the technology's sponsor. How does an agency decide
to launch a new development program? Who decides within
the agency? Who influences it from outside? The agency is a
decision unit, but the agency is also part of a larger process of
decision. Ultimately, decisions are made at the national policy
level by the President and Congress. They usually begin with
administrative judgments that a given technology should be
developed. An agency decides, in the context of other policy
actors, what it thinks it ought to do in accord with what *can
be*. What can be is determined by administrative judgments
of political as well as technical feasibility.

In many ways a development program is no different from
any other large-scale federal effort. It is pursued in accord
with a policy, i.e., a set of broad goals and objectives. This is
preceded usually by a certain degree of planning and lobbying for the policy. Policy is activated through programs. To
have meaning, programs must be implemented.[4]

INITIATING TECHNOLOGY

The decision to start a major technological program is an
important national policy decision. The significance of such
a decision for the agency in question can be immense. In the
case of the Department of Defense, for example:

. . . such program decisions occupy a crucial position, not only
in the weapons acquisition process, but in national security policy. They are the major strategic decisions of modern warfare,

4. On the general subject of implementation in relationship to policy, see
Jeffrey L. Pressman and Aaron R. Wildavsky, *Implementation* (Berkeley: University of California Press, 1974).

since past program decisions define for substantial periods of time the tactics that can be pursued by the armed forces.[5]

Such decisions usually do not get made without considerable effort on the part of a technology's proponents. The process by which that decision does get made may take months or even years. It generally begins when an individual or group, inside or outside government, perceives the desirability for a particular technology and begins advocating the innovation to a given prospective agency sponsor. It ends when the agency agrees to launch a development effort. Between these stages, a variety of activities takes place, most of which resemble more an effort at coalition-building by groups for and against particular technologies than a rational search for solutions to public problems. The importance of a particular technological choice is due not only to the nature of the technology chosen, but also to the fact that such choices utilize scarce resources and, therefore, close off alternative options. The resistances to a given program decision within and outside an agency are, thus, not necessarily "barriers to innovation." The resistances may be barriers to bad ideas.

There are a number of factors that influence the contest between advocates and opponents of big technology projects. They relate to the capacity of the organization to seek or receive proposals for technological ventures, the resistance on the part of the agency to certain ideas or certain proposers, and the power and strategies of those promoting or opposing particular technologies.

ORGANIZATIONAL CAPACITY

It is customary to use such terms as "ready" or "ripe" in reference to a given technology. A technology is "ready" for development or "ripe" for application. Similar terms may be

5. Merton Peck and Frederic Scherer, *The Weapons Acquisition Process: An Economic Analysis* (Cambridge: Harvard University Press, 1962), p. 225.

applied to administration and to policy. One reason many ideas for development are not funded is that there is a lack of interest or a capacity for doing so at the administrative level. This administrative reticence may be, in turn, a reflection of the agency's uncertain policy and political insecurity.

In 1966 the House Committee on Government Operations issued a report that compared the relative abilities of various agencies to deal with R&D. As might be expected, it found that such sectors as defense, space, and atomic energy not only spent considerable funds but also employed imaginative decision-makers who aggressively sought new ideas and then tried to develop new technology for the purpose of increasing the effectiveness of the overall programs. In contrast, it found such fields as urban transportation, housing, and hospital construction sadly lacking in the capacity either to receive or to use new technological concepts and products. Their R&D programs were small in scale, piecemeal in approach, diffuse in character, and largely non-developmental. More importantly, what R&D they did promote tended to have little effect on improving the effectiveness of the host agency's programs.[6]

Clearly, certain agencies are ahead of others in respect to organizational capacity to deal with R&D, particularly the management of large-scale development programs. It may be that such agencies have organizational purposes that are more identified with technological goals—or can be made so with relative ease. The less capable agencies often have more diffuse goals, even when these have a very large technological component, for example, urban mass transit.

Administrative underdevelopment, however, is not simply a function of the "social" agencies. Many potential technology-intensive agencies are quite unintensive about their R&D programs. Until the Arabs made energy supply a high national priority, there was a wide gap between the Atomic Energy Commission and various other agencies concerned with

6. U.S. House, Committee on Government Operations, *op. cit.*, p. 26.

non-nuclear sources insofar as R&D were concerned. At the outset of the 1970's, 86 percent of all federal energy R&D funds that had been spent since World War II had gone to AEC.[7] It was no wonder that advocates of development in solar, geothermal, or even coal energy felt that they were at a tremendous disadvantage vis-à-vis proponents of nuclear energy. AEC was buttressed by a network of laboratories, contractors, and university centers. The other energy "options" were backed by small, weak, sometimes newly created administrative units.

In 1974, in the midst of the energy crisis, legislation brought a new administrative entity, the Energy Research and Development Administration, into existence. It had a clear mandate to provide a more balanced government market for non-nuclear ideas in energy R&D. Before significant innovation could be expected in non-nuclear sectors, there would have to be administrative development in the techno-science agencies responsible for them. The capacity of the public as well as the private organizations behind the promotion of new technology is a subject too often ignored by students of science and technology policy. Organizational capacity should not be seen as reflecting upon the dedication or intelligence of individuals in underdeveloped agencies. It is, in part, a derivative of the environment of the agency and its general bureaucratic power. Power in administration depends on the agency's legislative and clientele support. Without such support, agencies will not build the machinery from which major R&D efforts can be launched. To develop administrative capacity, the power base of an agency must, therefore, first be strengthened. Only then can the agency attract and hold capable personnel and give them the base for accomplishing complex technical and managerial tasks. Capacity, because it does rest on power, must also be carefully

7. Claude E. Barfield, "Science Report/Nuclear Establishment Wins Commitment to Speed Development of Breeder Reactor," *National Journal* July 17, 1971, p. 1494.

controlled.[8] There can be administrative *over*development. In those cases, organizations will initiate technology programs, not necessarily because of national need, but out of organizational routine.

ORGANIZATIONAL RESISTANCE

Truly new or radical innovations are organizational as well as technological breakthroughs. They open up new territory in bureaucracy and also in science and technology. They upset existing status systems and internal power structures within organizations.[9] Many changes are forced which the organizational elites would prefer not to witness since the changes may directly threaten *them*. Even the most technology-intensive agencies tend to fear radical innovations. Second- and third-generation technological systems are harnessed to bureaucratic standard operating procedures, but the first system had to break new ground in an agency. Donald Schon has called the resistance of organizations to innovations "dynamic conservatism."[10] The resistance is not born wholly of bureaucratic inertia. It is based, in part, on fear and tends to be active—dynamic.

Agencies supposedly search for ideas that help them to solve their problems. They screen the many technological proposals coming to them, presumably in terms of mission, that is, "the business we are in." Even so, search and screening may be limited. What fits the mission may be circumscribed, not by the legislative mandate but by the inclinations of bureaucrats. It is not just the nature of the innovation that causes problems

8. For some thoughtful comments on the ingredients of bureaucratic power, see Francis Rourke, "Variations in Agency Power," in Francis Rourke, ed., *Bureaucratic Power in National Politics*, 2nd edition (Boston: Little, Brown, 1972), pp. 240–62.

9. Tom Burns and G. M. Stalker, *The Management of Innovation* (London: Tavistock, 1961), p. 6.

10. Donald Schon, *Beyond the Stable State* (New York: Random House, 1971), chap. 2.

in organizational acceptance. It is *who* is advocating the particular concept. An idea that might possibly be acceptable if it comes from quarters deemed credible by the organization might not be acceptable if it derives from "outsiders." The "N.I.H." (not-invented-here) factor operates in the decisions of agencies as to which technologies to develop and which to ignore.

A useful example is the Weather Bureau's resistance to cloud-seeding technology in the early days of weather modification.[11] The Weather Bureau was dominated by a particular scientific/professional estate—the meteorologists. The cloud-seeding concept came not only from outside the Bureau but also from a profession external to that with which most Bureau members identified. That a Nobel Laureate, Irving Langmuir, was the principal advocate of cloud-seeding mattered little to the Bureau. He was a physical chemist, not a meteorologist. That he attacked some of meteorology's pet theories in the process of proclaiming the coming of weather modification mattered more. The harder he pushed the Bureau and chided meteorologists, the harder the agency resisted. To the extent that weather modification was developed at all, following the initial demonstration of the technology in 1946–47, the credit is due the military agencies and the private sector. The "appropriate" agency, the Weather Bureau, had rejected the opportunity to develop the technology.

In the case of cloud-seeding, the technology was radical in its potential impact. Langmuir said that cloud-seeding would make it easier to change the weather than to predict it. In fact, he regarded as impossible the quest of the Weather Bureau and meteorologists for long-range predictions. Langmuir was out to change the "business" of the Weather Bureau. He was interested in altering the paradigm of meteorology. Such

11. W. H. Lambright, "Government and Technological Innovation: Weather Modification as a Case in Point," *Public Administration Review*, January/ February 1972.

radical changes were bound to be resisted by the human targets of Langmuir's efforts, especially when the moving force for change was an "outsider."

Technoscience agencies may innovate, but they tend to do so selectively, along established lines, and in ways that least threaten dominant organizational elites. In view of the number of bad or self-serving ideas proposed to agencies, such "dynamic conservatism" is a healthy screen, provided it does not go too far. Because of its existence, the power and strategies of advocates of new technology become key variables in administrative decisions to launch programs.

POWER AND STRATEGIES

Technological advocates can be outside or inside an organization. If outside, they can be "below" in universities, in industry, or in an agency's own laboratories. They can be "above" in the Executive Office of the President or in Congress. Ideas that are advocated come from many places. Most derive from the technical community, either in response to a perceived organizational need or to a technocrat's desire to promote a favored technological solution regardless of its match with an organizational problem. They converge on the agency that will have responsibility for funding the development program. Nevertheless, some ideas come with more political power behind them than others.

During World War II, on an emergency basis, leverage on the military agencies for the development of new technology was institutionalized in the Executive Office through the Office of Scientific Research and Development. Not only could OSRD rely on Presidential help to exert influence on the military in behalf of particular new weapons programs, but also, if the military proved recalcitrant, it had the authority and funds to develop the technology itself. The atomic bomb project began with a letter from Albert Einstein to the President. Machinery was set in motion at the very top of government. OSRD developed the weapon to a point where its feasibility was assured and *then* handed it on to the Army for further R&D and eventual deployment.

This kind of top-down decision-making is not the norm in federal technology policy. OSRD lasted only for the duration of the war. Agencies are jealous of their technical prerogatives. End-runs are possible, particularly when there are scientists in influential positions near the President. The professional linkages, between technical advocates at one level and science advisers to the President at another, have enabled more than one technology program to get under way. The problem with the end-run, top-down strategy is that it tends to be more effective in program initiation than in program implementation. If agencies feel that they are being asked to fund a new technology in which they have no interest, they may well drag their feet in implementing the program. The capacity of bureaucrats to sabotage a Presidential priority is well known.

Much more effective, as leverage on an agency over the long haul, is backing for a concept at the congressional subsystem level. The committee is outside the agency but inside the administrative policy network. When a congressional committee, with power over an agency's survival and growth, becomes the advocate of a particular technology, the agency usually acquiesces. Often, in fact, congressional pressure on an agency to develop a new technology is an external manifestation of an internal advocacy. Such appeals to Congress from within agencies arise because the process of R&D decision-making inside the agencies may be very slow, and advocates of new technology tend to be exceedingly impatient individuals.

Vincent Davis has described the process of launching technology programs within the Navy. Tracing the politics of innovation from the time a Navy official decides to champion a new system to the point at which the organization makes the decision to launch a program as an agency goal, Davis reveals a complex process of bureaucratic alliance building.[12] The advocate in this case is an "insider," but he begins in a minority position.

The inside advocate's first political technique is to "enlist supporters from among friends and colleagues at his own rank level." This constitutes what Davis calls a "horizontal political alliance." This group then seeks "vertical" allies—allies high up enough to commit organizational resources to initial exploratory work. (In the Navy, as with most high-capacity agencies, there usually is money for exploratory development leading to a feasibility basis for programmatic decision.) Such a "coordinate political alliance" would seem essential in any inside-generated innovation.

The principal argument used by the inside-innovating coalition is *not* that the technology represents a new conception in international politics, long-range military strategy, or the like. Inside advocates, usually being middle-level bureaucrats, tend not to speak in such broad strategic terms. They merchandise their technology within the organization as a better way to perform some well-established Navy task or mission. They certainly do not emphasize a technology's "radical" nature—even if it is of that variety. The technology is put forward as a solution to an existing "performance gap."[13]

The push from innovators inevitably runs into resistance. Davis found that, in the Navy, the coalition pattern of opposition usually is the reverse of that for the innovation. That is, higher officers seek to thwart the innovating coalition, and their rank is usually sufficient to bring aboard some allies, automatically, from below. Their opposition, at least at this early stage in the technology's development, usually is based primarily on budgetary factors. They argue that the organization has enough programs going and that there is little reason

12. Vincent Davis, "The Politics of Innovation: Patterns in Navy Cases," in Richard G. Head and Ervin J. Rokke, eds., *American Defense Policy*, 3rd edition (Baltimore: Johns Hopkins University Press, 1973), pp. 391–406.
13. *Ibid.*, p. 405.

to initiate yet another new system. Like the innovating coalition, those against (at the higher ranks of the Navy) argue in Navy performance terms and do not consider broad implications for international politics, relations with the Soviet Union, and so forth.[14]

Which coalition wins often depends upon which is more persistent. Since the opposition tends to have greater hierarchical authority, the innovating coalition may have no choice but to go outside. Since such a move carries risks for the insider, the actual lobbying may be carried out by prospective contractors who share the insiders' enthusiasm. One may assume that outside appeals are couched much more in traditional political/military strategic arguments than in the values of organizational effectiveness. There is great pressure within an agency, particularly in the military services, for a technical advocate not to go outside but to stay within the channels of the traditional chain of command. To follow such a course may mean slow progress, even death, for a project. Admiral Hyman Rickover, who fought a long, often bitter battle inside and outside the Navy on behalf of the first nuclear submarine, was apparently passed over for promotion as a "reward" for some of his tactics. As historians Richard Hewlett and Francis Duncan put it: "Rickover's tactics were to approach his assignment with ruthless determination and as a project manager to fight to the last for everything he needed to attain his goal. These tactics, admirable in a project manager, were precisely what appeared to many to disqualify Rickover for 'broader' responsibilities."[15] Congress rescued him, but the Navy made its point.

The more radical the innovation and the greater the potential expense, the higher will be the organizational risks. Hence, outside leverage is frequently needed by insiders to accomplish a program initiation. In some subsystems such

14. *Ibid.*
15. Hewlett and Duncan, *Nuclear Navy, 1946–1962* (Chicago: University of Chicago Press, 1974), p. 191.

outside support is readily obtainable. Some Congressmen are more technology-oriented than the agencies that they supervise. In other subsystems, however, congressional conservatism may be extreme and serve to dampen rather than to excite technocratic cravings for innovation. Whatever the case, program decisions invariably take time because they require resolution of problems and overcoming of political obstacles within the agency. New technologies not only produce change for society but also foment change for the "little society" that is the agency responsible for their development. That is why successful advocates of new technology in bureaucratic settings tend to play down the newness factor. The performance-gap argument is a conservative strategy. The technology, it is held, will merely permit the organization to do its traditional job better. In this way, strategies as well as technologies are subjugated to administrative routines.

NATIONAL PROGRAM DECISION

The program initiation phase may be conceived as a relationship between those advocating a particular technological program and the public organization from whose budget the funds to develop the technology must come. In this sense, it is a "seller/buyer" relationship. Once the organizational buyer has made its decision favorable to a technology (a program decision), it must then become the advocate to its administrative and congressional superiors. The agency acts as an official interest group. The interest around which it mobilizes is the technological program.

The politics/administration dichotomy would argue: the President and Congress decide; agencies execute. But what Presidents and Congress decide may be based on plans put forward by their "neutral tools." "Where you stand depends on where you sit." From the agency's perspective, *its* program decision ends the initiation phase. What happens thereafter, including obtaining the necessary approvals, is implementation. From the perspective of national political bodies, however, an administrative decision is but a plan for action which can be approved, disapproved, or delayed. For them, implementation follows decision at the top. Agencies need topside decisions. Such decisions provide certainty in a highly precarious political environment. Decisions can be made at the agency level; but, without the necessary program approvals and funds from above, agencies may drift and development programs may lag. Agencies live by what they do, and what they do is execute programs. They also care about what they do. In particular, the chief career professionals of agencies care. If agencies do development work, they must propose new technology programs. Whether what they ultimately do is what they had planned depends upon political decisions from above. It may be very difficult to *get* the necessary political decisions, even with the help of subsystem allies.

Thus, NASA proposed to go to the moon long before such plans were made national policy. As John Logsdon has stated in his study, *The Decision To Go to the Moon:*

. . . operating pretty much in a political vacuum in terms of policy guidance, and basing their choice on what constituted a rational technical program of manned space flight development, NASA planners chose a lunar landing objective fully two years before President Kennedy announced his choice of the lunar landing as a national goal.[16]

Without the 1961 national decision, NASA no doubt would have continued to press, as it had since 1959, for the lunar decision. It might even have begun implementing its decision as it could, incrementally. This is not to argue that there is a technological or bureaucratic determinism. It is simply to point out that there are levels of decision in national government. Where there is a policy vacuum, agencies will partially fill the gap. Moreover, political decision-making, especially in

16. Logsdon, *The Decision To Go to the Moon* (Cambridge: MIT Press, 1970), pp. 56, 57.

science and technology matters, is dependent upon facts as to capabilities generated by the administrative branch and R&D experts. What politicians may view as capability assessments cannot be separated (at least when presented by agencies) from the agencies' goals and objectives.

NASA had plenty of help in obtaining the Apollo decision. Agencies usually do have assistance in getting support for their major development projects. Congressional committees and R&D clientele, generally, do have vested interests in the continuance of the administrative function with which they are related. Thus, Representative Chet Holifield was the principal advocate on behalf of the Liquid Metal Fast Breeder Reactor. In 1971 this was approved as the nation's leading energy R&D project by President Nixon, following a lengthy lobbying effort by the project's proponents. At least since 1967, it had been the top priority project of AEC/JCAE.[17] A longtime nuclear enthusiast and onetime chairman of the Joint Committee on Atomic Energy, Holifield was heading the House Government Operations Committee in 1971. He was strategically located to block a major federal reorganization that President Nixon wanted very much. No project could have had a more devoted congressional spokesman than the Breeder had in Holifield. As he stated at the time:

I'm 67 and may well not be around when this program is completed. But my main goal before I hang up my gloves is to see that it is well funded and organized and backed with a clear national commitment.[18]

The sequence of events in the Apollo and the Breeder Reactor decisions, insofar as administrative/political relations are concerned, is not unique. It is the norm for "accelerated" technologies—those that gain high priority or become "crash"

17. Allen L. Hammond, "The Fast Breeder Reactor: Signs of a Critical Reaction," *Science*, Vol. 176, April 1972, p. 391.
18. Claude E. Barfield, "Science Report/Nuclear Establishment Wins Commitment to Speed Development of Breeder Reactor," *National Journal*, July 17, 1971, p. 1496.

programs through a conscious national decision. Even where accelerated technologies are not at issue, such persuasion and bargaining between subsystem levels and national levels of policy are typical. Technoscience agencies and their subsystem allies propose, and the President and Congress dispose, with more or less controversy, depending upon the nature and the scale of the technology.

Most development programs simply appear in the President's budget under the appropriate agency and are approved, with modest changes, by Congress. They go from agency projects to national projects, quietly and unobtrusively. Costs, at least during the initial year, are minimal. Publicity accompanies only the biggest and most controversial programs. The President makes technology visible to a broader national audience by publicly associating his own prestige with that of the program. A technoscience agency likes nothing more than Presidential commitment. Through such decisions, agency goals become national objectives.

A Presidential decision to initiate a program commits not only the President but also others in government. Such a commitment may matter most within the Executive Office of the President. Following President Nixon's 1972 decision to support NASA's Space Shuttle Program, the Office of Management and Budget,* an adversary of the Shuttle up to that time, suddenly began "cooperating." A Presidential decision usually helps to obtain congressional support. Although many programs are launched without overt Presidential backing, those that have it are advantaged. Whether deliberate and visible or relatively unconscious and unnoticed, decisions at the Presidential and national levels are more than mere affirmations to agency plans. They are the means of legitimating administrative policy in a democratic society. They are also important to the process by which the technoscience agencies move their programs forward.

---

* In 1970 the Bureau of the Budget was renamed the Office of Management and Budget.

Developing Technology

"A program," say Pressman and Wildavsky, "consists of governmental action initiated in order to secure objectives whose attainment is problematical."[19] Few programs are more problematical than those of R&D. If the only barriers with which agencies had to contend were technological, these alone would cause headaches. But the hurdles to implementation that are political lead to even more serious uncertainties. Indeed, in federally funded development projects, it is extremely difficult to separate the technological from the political barriers affecting the course of programs.

From beginning to end, programs are implemented in a political environment. Political opposition can serve to enlarge the technological barriers by creating more stringent design specifications as the price of acceptance, while political support can remove technological barriers by easing the performance requirements. Technology and politics interact throughout the development cycle. To cope with the politics of technological development, agencies employ a variety of strategies and tactics aimed at securing the necessary support. The first strategy is to maintain cohesion so that the agency does not defeat its own purposes through internal bickering. The second is to build support from external groups, particularly those that control the allocation of resources.

MAINTAINING INTERNAL SUPPORT

Just because a decision is made to launch a program by an agency and is ratified by higher executive authority does not mean the bureaucratic struggle has ended. The battle for programs and priorities within and between agencies continues. A program that is in the interest of the Navy, for example, may be antagonistic to the needs of the Air Force. What may suit a Secretary of Defense may not please any of the services. A decision favoring the civilian space program can injure the

19. Pressman and Wildavsky, *op. cit.,* p. xiv.

military space program. Given scarce resources for new development programs, decisions will invariably help or hurt various interests within the executive branch. There is thus a constant struggle, *after* national program decisions, to recoup losses or reverse unfavorable decisions. It is not unknown for one agency to discredit a rival agency's capacity to run a development program, particularly if it wants that program itself.

With so much competition among the agencies, with many enemies (real or imagined) outside the executive branch, agencies charged with particular development missions strive to present a united front to the outside world. This may involve tactics such as *suppressing or containing dissent* within the boundaries of the agency. Administrative leaders wish to protect a large-scale development program from factions within the agency. Ironically, one of the major ways of accomplishing this is to protect the agency from the development programs. A tactic for doing so comes under the heading of *"moderation."*[20] Moderation means sacrificing short-term gains for long-term support.[21]

The problem that the large-scale technology program presents an agency is that its very size makes it a threat to other efforts within the agency, as well as to the agency's top leaders. A big technology program can devour the resources of the sponsor. The project managers of large-scale technology tend to be single-minded, energetic, and ambitious men who are true believers in the importance of the program. They tend to view criticisms as either irrelevant or mischievous. They may trample upon other agency programs and make end-runs around the top agency officials unless somehow they are kept "in bounds."

20. Harvey Sapolsky found moderation, co-optation, differentiation, and management innovation four means used by Polaris managers to implement their program, in his study *The Polaris System Development: Bureaucratic and Programmatic Success in Government* (Cambridge: Harvard University Press, 1972). I have adapted and extended these four categories, and included additional strategies and tactics as well, for the purposes of this chapter.

21. *Ibid.*, p. 54.

This is especially true in the early phases of implementation. High-priority national projects often have a honeymoon period, just as do Presidents. For a relatively short time (perhaps a few years), criticism may be slight, and oversight by such entities as the Office of Management and Budget, Congress, or the General Accounting Office may be minimal. Project managers and their agencies have an opportunity to "cash in" during this period of permissive administrative and political overview.

Project managers usually try to get what they can get while they can get it, but the tactic of moderation calls for some measure of self-denial for longer-term interests. Such a restrained use of the honeymoon period may well be one of the less comfortable tactics from a technoscience agency's perspective and certainly from that of a particular project manager who would be most affected. Those closest to the project, for example, tend to be so performance-oriented that they resent any notion of "under-innovation" in order to save costs on development. They resist reprogramming "surplus" money to other agency enterprises. In the case of Apollo, this problem came up early. It involved:

. . . a bitter falling out with D. Brainerd Holmes, an able young RCA executive whom [James] Webb [NASA administrator] hired in 1961 to boss the manned space-flight effort. The battle was complicated by an internal power struggle among Holmes and other top officers, eventually including Webb, and the showdown came on the most fundamental NASA problem . . . the danger that the burgeoning Apollo program might drain NASA resources as to undercut such critical scientific research as unmanned interplanetary probes and space applications programs. Holmes pressed so hard for $400 million in additional funds for Apollo that Webb appealed to President Kennedy and got him to kill the proposal. . . .[22]

22. "Now It's an Agonizing Reappraisal of the Moon Race," *Fortune*, November 1963, p. 21.

The agency needs hard-driving managers for its lead programs, but the programs require the help of the agency for their long-term success. That means that they need the support of other programs and, particularly, the agency's top leadership. Unless an agency can master itself, it is unlikely to be able to influence favorably the forces in its environment whose support it must have to see any problem through to successful completion. Hence, the need for moderation, whether imposed from above or accepted voluntarily by large-scale programs.

Moderation tactics vary beyond the purely financial and power issues implied by the Apollo case. They extend even to dress and other bureaucratic perquisites. The managers of Polaris, the project to develop a missile-launching capability for atomic-powered submarines, tried to avoid any connotation of their being an "elite" group within the Navy by taking modest quarters in Washington and avoiding special uniforms and insignias. Here, the long-term support that Polaris managers were hopefully purchasing through their policies of moderation was with their colleagues in the Navy with whom they and Polaris would have to live, indefinitely.[23] Such self-denial is not taken in the interests of altruism but in the interests of bureaucratic survival. It is difficult to overestimate the importance of maintaining support within the host agency as a general strategy for development. Cohesion is prerequisite to externally directed bureaucratic aims.

MAINTAINING EXTERNAL SUPPORT

Since large-scale technology programs must continue for often a decade or more to reach completion and since the political environment can change radically during that time, it becomes essential for technical success, that the agency create a favorable and relatively stable set of relationships with external resource-supplying groups. A number of tactics may be

23. Sapolsky, *The Polaris System Development, op. cit.,* pp. 55, 56.

employed in support of this overall strategy: co-optation, differentiation, packaging/repackaging, and image-building.

Co-optation was given prominence as a bureaucratic tactic by Philip Selznick. It involved the "absorption of nucleuses of power into the administrative structure of an organization." The purpose of doing so was to make "possible the elimination or appeasement of potential sources of opposition." Co-optation could mean the actual sharing of power, or it could merely stand as a symbol of such sharing. Federal agencies, like all organizations, would prefer not to share power if they can help it. Sharing, as Selznick showed, can have its cost in organizational goals. As the "price of accommodation, the organization commits itself to avenues of activity and lines of policy enforced by the character of the co-opted elements."[24]

Compromise and sharing may be essential, however, if the agency is to carry out its program at all. In some projects, there is probably more sharing of power with non-governmental interests, particularly with the contractors performing the R&D work, than with "official" sources of power. Subsystem legislators lack the time to penetrate the technical details of large-scale development administration, but they do want to be kept informed. Agencies fail to keep legislative constituents informed at their peril. What they generally do, therefore, is to try to accent the positive in testimony before Congress. When questions are asked, they answer them truthfully, but they do not volunteer information detrimental to their program. They keep subsystem legislators informed, but the information tends to be on the favorable side.

A subtle but probably most effective means of co-opting legislators is to link their interests with those of the project through the selection of contractors. Contracting-out provides enormous flexibility for a technoscience agency, in selecting companies in the districts of key legislative constituents. Locational politics can be used by the agency to enlarge the program's geographical, legislative clientele. Contracts and subcontracts combine the interests of regional economies, unions, industry, and legislators with those of the program. The award of contracts makes for political support through economic dependency. Government-by-contract is co-optation by another name. It purchases legislative loyalty without necessarily increasing congressional scrutiny into Executive decision-making. Indeed, it usually leads to less oversight. Congressmen are anxious for the project to survive; they do not want to cause problems (at least so long as the project appears to be running smoothly). Thus, do pork-barrel politics mix with new technology.

Federal agencies also seek to co-opt another important segment of their overall constituency—the scientific community. The relatively apolitical stance that scientists generally have in the minds of the political estate can be used by scientists as they seek to influence policy, but it can also be used by technoscience agencies. The scientific endorsement of an agency's program can reassure non-technical legislators and Executive Office personnel. Scientists are, thus, appointed to advisory boards, given research grants, and otherwise involved in a development program. At the beginning, during the planning phase of implementation, they may well share power, given the technical uncertainties that have to be surmounted and the need to choose among various technical paths.[25] Once under way, the career elites in the agency take charge. While they may continue to use scientific advisers, they tend to listen most to those who reinforce views already held.

Yet another group which the agency seeks to co-opt is the user of the technological product being created. More will be said on the agency-user linkage in the following chapter. Suf-

25. On scientists in planning, see Leonard Sayles and Margaret Chandler, *Managing Large Systems: Organizations for the Future* (New York: Harper and Row, 1971), Chapter 3.

fice it to say here, users are key elements of the agency's environment. They constitute external demand. An agency tries to maximize user support while minimizing user "interference" in the actual administration of the program. In Polaris, the project organization had to contend with intraorganizational users—the submariners—who were not especially enthusiastic about adding missiles to "their" submarines. The development people avoided outright opposition on the part of the submariners by altering certain aspects of the weapons system design, even though these alterations were not technically required.[26] This was a modest sharing of power, or at least acquiescence, on the part of the development project group in exchange for user support.

Finally, there is the President and the question of how to co-opt him. The best way to begin has already been mentioned, i.e., by obtaining a Presidential endorsement of a program as a national goal. But Presidents come and go. Development may take a long time. How is the *Presidency* co-opted? Are there some interests that are peculiarly Presidential, that can garner White House support, year after year, regardless of who sits in the Oval Office? It would appear that appeals to Presidential concerns for foreign policy are useful—whether they are related to international competition or cooperation.

As long as NASA was racing the Russians to the moon in the 1960's, the agency had the President as a primary constituent. Once the race was "won," the agency endeavored to tie its programs to Presidential interests of the 1970's, such as détente and global interdependence. Instead of competing, the U.S. and the U.S.S.R. began "cooperating" in a joint space mission. Moreover, NASA's primary project, the Space Shuttle, was scheduled to carry into orbit a space lab created by a consortium of European governments. Any problem that would impact on the Shuttle would create problems for the

26. Harvey Sapolsky, "The Bureaucratic Politics of Large-Scale Technological Projects," Paper: American Association for the Advancement of Science, December 26–31, 1970.

President in his foreign relations. This would be true for any President. "Foreign entanglements" may be helpful to technoscience agencies, especially when domestic political support appears to be eroding, but they are not always guarantees for the security of large-scale programs. DOD's Skybolt (a missile-carrying airplane) was "shot down" by Secretary of Defense McNamara in spite of the fact that one of its major users was to be America's chief ally, Great Britain.[27]

No bureaucratic strategy or tactic is foolproof. However, as a means for assuring long-term support from the Presidential Office, as contrasted with a specific individual, technoscience agencies are learning the benefits of an active foreign policy. Most R&D-intensive agencies do have their own "little State Departments." International cooperation can sometimes help, almost as much as international competition, to keep large-scale programs going. "Alliance politics"[28] can become a powerful tactic in the hands of an agency.

Differentiation refers to "attempts by organizations to establish unchallengeable claims on valued resources by distinguishing their own products or programs from those of their competitors." It aims at "creating identities that are unique and favorable in the view of those who control resource allocation."[29] Differentiation is used by agencies to get political support for program initiation, and it is also used to help them implement their programs.

In the early days of Polaris, the Navy frequently had to justify its role in missiles work. It had to explain why its missile system was different from, or superior to, that of the Air Force. The Air Force, for its part, has had a similar problem with respect to airplanes. The question is raised: "Why do we need strategic airplanes, such as the B1 Bomber, in an age of ballistic missiles?" Differentiation can be employed at various times during the course of a development program. It may

27. On the cancellation of Skybolt, see Richard Neustadt, *Alliance Politics* (New York and London: Columbia University Press, 1970).

28. *Ibid.*

29. Sapolsky, *The Polaris System Development, op. cit.*, pp. 43, 44.

even change or reverse an earlier program decision that was unfavorable to a given technology.

An agency may merge its interests with those of a rival organization in order to obtain a national program decision in the first place. As soon as actual development begins, however, the agency renews its attempt to obtain independence. From the point of view of the agency, technology is being optimized by separate programs; so is organizational interest. Before a program is complete, a joint effort may long since have given way to separate and "differentiated" activities. The Navy's Polaris program began as an appendage to the ongoing Army Jupiter Missiles Project. In the end, Jupiter was killed, and Polaris emerged as one of the principal strategic systems on which America was to build its defense policy.

Similarly, the Navy never went along with Secretary of Defense McNamara's notion of commonality when it came to the TFX airplane.[30] It contested the McNamara policy throughout the development phase. Eventually, once it was assured that an alternative tactical fighter closer to Navy requirements would be available, it allowed friends in Congress to kill the Navy version of TFX. One plane could not serve the interests of both the Air Force and the Navy (or so the services argued). Differentiation as a tactic implies that a given organization's requirements are absolutely unique and cannot be compromised in any way. Differentiation is one way that an agency preserves its claim to a piece of administrative action. The Navy has every intention of remaining independent of the Air Force in respect to tactical air power. It has no trouble differentiating its needs from those of sister agencies.

As a corollary to differentiation, there is the tactic of *packaging/repackaging*. As national priorities change, the initial reasons that impelled Congress and the President to support a particular program may become less critical. The agency in

---

30. See Robert J. Art, *The TFX Decision: McNamara and the Military* (Boston: Little, Brown, 1968). During the implementation stage, the TFX airplane's name was changed to F-111.

charge of the program finds that it must discover ways to make its effort appear "relevant" to new priorities as they arise. It can change the program, but, if it believes the program is still viable, it may change the appearance, or package, of the program without really altering the content. NASA has found ways to relate some of its space programs to national security, ecology, and, most recently, energy. The programs stay the same, but the way they are packaged and repackaged moves with the times.

This point, concerning appearance and reality in big technology programs, points up administrative *image-building* as a tactic. Such image-building is especially important in creating the belief on the part of others that an agency has competence. Politicians may not understand the intricacies of science and technology, but they do think that they know poor management when they see it. Hence, an agency must persuade those who control the funds on which its program depends that all is well with the way it is running that program. Government depends on trust. For example, it depends on trust by Congress in the subsystem committees that overview the agencies; trust by the committees in the agencies that they supervise; and trust by agencies in the project organizations that are specifically charged with developing technologies. How does an agency convince non-technical, elected officials that it is managing a large-scale technology program well? As the "middle man" between R&D and democratic political institutions, an agency has a special role in the hierarchy of mutual confidence on which technology programs are built.

Merely seeming to be concerned with "management" helps. Being "innovative" in management is even better. If an agency can show that it is as creative in running a program as it is in developing hardware, it is well on its way to winning friends in Congress and the Executive Office. "Management innovation" was central to Polaris. The leaders of Polaris achieved considerable autonomy by introducing managerial techniques that gave the impression of managerial competence to outsiders. Sapolsky's close inspection of Polaris, however, revealed a surprising fact about these managerial techniques:

PERT [Program Evaluation and Review Technique], PERT/COST, the management information center and a dozen other well known management techniques were invented or developed by the Program. Whenever there was a question on POLARIS' development status or the like, program officials always had a colored chart, a slide, or a computer printout which would demonstrate the effectiveness of the management team. Actually, this strategy might well be labelled the "Slight of Hand Strategy" since few of these management techniques were ever used to manage the POLARIS development. The use of PERT in the program, for example, was strongly opposed by those technical officers who were in charge of the development effort and there never was a complete application of the technique in the program, but the illusion of PERT's use was carefully cultivated. During most critical stages of the POLARIS development when PERT's role was minimal, the program held hundreds of briefings and prepared thousands of booklets describing how PERT was guiding the missile's progress. The message was that no one need be concerned about the quality of the program's development decisions as the program itself was the pioneer in perfecting management systems for complex projects. And since enough people who could influence policy believed this to be the case, the program was able to gain the independence and flexibility it needed to deal effectively with the missile's technological uncertainties.[31]

If Polaris was well-managed, as most observers have argued, it was not because of the management techniques to which its success was attributed. Indeed, it is difficult to pin down any standards for a well-managed technological program. Usually, when a project is completed within cost, on time, and in a manner that leaves the user of the product satisfied, it is called

31. Harvey Sapolsky, "The Bureaucratic Politics of Large-Scale Technological Projects," *op. cit.* In his book on Polaris, Sapolsky elaborates on this use or non-use of PERT. See Sapolsky, *The Polaris System Development, op. cit.*, chap. 4.

a success. One symptom of "bad" management is the cost-over-run, but, even here, appearances are deceiving. Cost-overruns may not be overruns at all but *realistic* costs of a program whose original estimates were unduly optimistic.

Apollo shares with Polaris the glory of being a "well-run," large-scale program in terms of avoiding an overrun. But how did NASA avoid such an overrun in a $24 billion program? By some miraculous management techniques? To be sure, NASA pioneered many management innovations and willingly offered itself for study as a showcase for "project management" at its optimum.

NASA, because of the high priority of Apollo, was able to avoid an overrun by estimating *realistically*. Hence, when Apollo came in at a figure which was approximately that suggested almost a decade before, NASA was heralded for its "good management." Good management, in this case, was merely cost realism in an environment in which costs were not a very important consideration in the decision to initiate Project Apollo. The pace of the program was far more important to President Kennedy than was the cost.[32]

This is not to suggest that Polaris and Apollo were not well run. The point is that standards for successful management are elusive and that the political environment may determine, far more than internal administrative genius, the conditions under which it is possible to be realistic as to costs and thus win a reputation for managerial efficiency. Projects with mod-

32. This point is well documented in Logsdon, *Decision To Go to the Moon, op. cit.* In 1958, he found, the Air Force estimated it could land a man on the moon by 1965 for $1.5 billion (p. 47). In 1959, the Army said that not only could it reach the moon by 1965, but it could also begin setting up a lunar base. For such a program, lasting from 1959 to 1967, the cost would be $6 billion (p. 52). There is the feeling of "competitive bidding" in these "optimistic" estimates. In contrast, Logsdon reports that, in April 1961, NASA Deputy Administrator Hugh Dryden gave President Kennedy a pessimistic estimate. Dryden said that the cost of beating the Russians to the moon might be as high as $40 billion, "and even so there was only an even chance of beating the Soviets." Kennedy indicated that the cost bothered him greatly, but declared: "There's nothing more important" (p. 106). See also, Hugh Sidey, *John F. Kennedy, President* (New York: Atheneum, 1964), pp. 121–23.

est political backing would have great difficulty in getting initiated, much less implemented, if their proponents were entirely "realistic" about their costs.

CONCLUSION

It takes a favorable political climate to start, much less to maintain, a large-scale public technology program. The technical uncertainties are often overshadowed by those of the political environment. Technologies depend on coalitions of support being superior to those in opposition to the innovation. Technoscience agencies initiate programs. Some agencies, however, are far more alert than others to opportunities and are more forceful in obtaining the necessary backing from central political authority.

Although representing government in its most innovative role, the technoscience agencies nevertheless reflect bureaucracy's inertial character. They tend to be biased toward evolutionary rather than discontinuous technology. It is usually difficult to win an agency's backing for a *new* development program. It may be impossible to do so if the program is seen as threatening change in existing power structures and status systems within the agency which is being asked to sponsor the technology. The "newer" the technology, the more likely outside pressure will have to be brought to bear on an agency to obtain an initiation decision.

Initiating technology is just that—a beginning. To complete a program requires implementation. There are two phases to implementation. The first, discussed in this chapter, is development. As shown, cohesion within an agency and a variety of bureaucratic strategies and tactics help to move the technology ahead. The second phase, discussed in the ensuing two chapters, is application. Applying a technology requires its deployment or, as it is often called, introduction. The development and application phases are closely linked. Just as there is always much research in development efforts, so the question of use is always present during the development period. R&D does indeed *phase* into operations, and technoscience agencies are often as involved in the effort to deploy new technology as to invent it. The "end" of an R&D program is the "start" of an applications effort. Where does a technoscience agency's control over the technology terminate and that of the applying organization commence—"late" in development or "early" in application? That is one of the chief questions that makes the implementation of technology especially difficult.

3

Deploying High Technology

TECHNOLOGIES ARE developed by the federal government to be deployed. Perhaps many scientists and engineers pursue technology for its own sake,[1] but government is *supposed* to have practical use as an eventual goal. This is certainly the mandate of so-called mission agencies. To an increasing extent, it is also the case for the National Science Foundation.[2] The R&D continuum assumes that the experimental will merge with the routine: development with operations.[3] The problem is that institutional interests, including those of technoscience agencies, may interfere with the system-wide goal of application and use. What is the nature of the interface between federally funded R&D and operations?

A technology may "work," but that does not necessarily mean it will be moved into operations. To be marketed, it must ordinarily be "pushed" by a technoscience agency or

1. Daedalus of New Scientist, "Pure Technology," in Albert H. Teich, ed., *Technology and Man's Future* (New York: St. Martin's Press, 1972).

2. The term "mission" is generally used to refer to agencies with missions other than the support of science per se. NSF does have a science-support mission by act of Congress, although, as is discussed in Chapter 6 below, even NSF supposedly supports science for "national" interests.

3. For a seminal discussion of the transfer of technology from development to use, on which the present study builds, see Leonard Sayles and Margaret Chandler, *Managing Large Systems: Organizations for the Future* (New York: Harper and Row, 1971), chap. 7.

"pulled" by user demand. In government-sponsored technology, bureaucratic power is a crucial variable in the deployment process. As a technology is transferred from development to use, so also is *control* over that technology. In the process, an R&D program may thus be lost by one agency, and an operational program may be gained by another agency. Even where deployment is not wholly interagency, administrative interests are involved. The more important the technology, the greater are an agency's own stakes in controlling the direction and pace of its deployment. The disposition of the technology (i.e., who *should* be the user) is also frequently a major question of public policy.

Users come in layers. Ultimately the people can be considered the users (if only indirectly) of publicly financed technology. As taxpayers they are certainly investors in such technologies. The role of the public, however, may be quite peripheral to deployment decision-making. This is especially the case in the advanced or "high technologies" of defense, space, and atomic energy. A myriad of user organizations stand between the technoscience agencies and the public. Some users are obviously much more important in the innovation process than others. Frequently, the technoscience agency identifies such key users itself. In other cases, the users make themselves known to the agency.

From the perspective of the technoscience agency, it is usually sufficient to denote the immediate (or target) users. These may be other federal agencies, state and local governments, manufacturing or service-providing industries. A technoscience agency shows by its actions those that it regards as its primary customers. The relationships between the technoscience agency and the users constitute the heart of an administrative system for deployment. The dynamics of such systems vary across the government. For example, in high technology sectors, the number of participants in deployment decision-making, other than the technology producers and users, tends to be relatively limited.

In high technology areas, technologies are often large in scale and esoteric in content. The technoscience agencies and users tend to be big and sophisticated. The general public is ordinarily represented only indirectly, to the extent that elected officials oversee the deployment process. While deployment takes place in a political environment, the politics is usually not macro. Great responsibility is placed upon the subsystems of government to represent the broadest possible public interest in new technology. Where they fail, macropolitics or a resort to the courts by disaffected citizens may be a consequence.

The administrative systems for application generally fall into three models. In one, power is *concentrated.* The agency that sponsors development (the technoscience agency) is also the user of its technology. In a second model, power is *federated.* There are at least two organizations involved in the process of application, and these two entities are independent of one another; that is, the government agency or department responsible for developing the technology must transfer the technology to another government agency or non-governmental organization responsible for its use. Relations between the two (or more) actors in the federated system involve considerable bargaining and negotiation. Finally, there is the *fragmented* system. Here, participants are many and control over deployment is widely dispersed. The fragmented system is discussed in the succeeding chapter. The present chapter deals with the concentrated and the federated systems.

Concentrated Power and Weapons Deployment

No administrative system of technology is deeper and, at the same time, narrower than that of the Department of Defense. At any given time, scores of new weapons systems are making their way from development to operations. Many are classified. The sheer size of the DOD budget for R&D (about $10 billion in FY 1976) makes overall review by the Office of Management and Budget (OMB), much less the President and Congress, an almost insurmountable challenge. There is simply not the time nor organized expertise outside the Pentagon to study all the weapons programs in detail. There is a tendency on the part of those external to DOD to focus on a few major weapons systems, leaving to the Secretary of Defense the primary duty of managing the totality of military technology. Still, no Secretary of Defense, given his many other responsibilities, can be expected to exercise an in-depth, across-the-board control over all that is developed and sought to be deployed in military technology. Inevitably, responsibility is delegated to the R&D and military professionals in the Pentagon and in the services. Doing so biases the system toward deployment in ways not found in less monolithic systems.

From the time a new weapons program is proposed until it makes its way into the military arsenal or goes down in a cancellation decision, it has champions who are from the developer and user sides of the organization.[4] Before a program decision is made by the Secretary of Defense the military estate must certify that it has a need for the system. The "requirements" system forces the potential user to consider the merits and demerits at an early point. Those technologies that are favored constitute a demand pull at the outset of the development process.

As the development proceeds, development personnel and the military may spend enormous amounts of time defending the program to the Secretary's office, OMB, and Congress. A partnership evolves. At the early stage, when much R&D is needed, the scientists and technologists may have the greater informal influence, but the military presence is always there. Usually, a military officer has hierarchical authority over a scientific/engineering group. As the technology moves closer to fruition, the military users take greater interest and command. They determine when the technology is operational.

4. Developers can, of course, also be formally outside the organization, in the industrial complex that supports DOD. Such contractors may be much closer to the power centers of the agency, however, than the agency's own civil service laboratories.

There is always a question of readiness, with R&D people usually conservative and anxious to make the last little improvement in engineering; however, a technology may be "ready enough" from the user's perspective. If the user is the core professional elite of the agency, the scientific and engineering estates go along.

"If a system works, and works well," former Secretary of Defense Robert McNamara has written, "there is strong pressure from many directions to procure and deploy the weapon out of all proportion to the prudent level required."[5] The pressures come at the end of R&D, not only from the users, but also from the contractors who wish to become manufacturers. The big money in weapons is to be made in procurement, not R&D. The R&D contractors, working with DOD technologists and the military, are in an excellent position to be the ones who get the procurement contracts. Their potentially dual role as developers *and* manufacturers creates a bias toward deployment. Thus, it is also to the advantage of Congressmen and Senators who represent districts that are receiving defense R&D contracts to push for deployment. To the extent that weapons sales to foreign nations aid in the U.S. balance-of-payments, this factor also pulls toward deployment. Such is the "pressure from many directions" of which McNamara wrote.

The problem with a concentrated system is that it works too well. The process of development and deployment becomes routinized. Few outside of or even high in the Pentagon are involved in key decisions along the way. Thus, much technology is developed that serves no useful military purpose, or it is procured in quantities far greater than needed, or it is deployed sooner than technically or politically wise. There is, to be sure, an urgency arising from the international environment, but there is also an urgency owing to the bureaucratization of science and technology. In a wartime set-

5. Robert McNamara, *The Essence of Security* (New York: Harper and Row, 1968), p. 196.

ting, the dangers of a concentrated system become most pronounced. With remarkable speed, a new technology can move from the laboratory to tests in the field to operational use. The most dramatic example of such an occurrence involved the atom bomb. More recently, the war in Southeast Asia provided new evidence of the facility with which uncertain technologies may be deployed as operational weapons. Consider the case of weather modification.

From 1966 to 1972, the Air Force and the Navy participated in extensive ($3.6 million-per-year) cloud-seeding tests and operations in Southeast Asia, with knowledge severely restricted to those with a "need to know."[6] So restricted, in fact, was the program that, apparently, even Secretary of Defense Laird did not know about the effort until after he had testified before Congress in 1972 that no such seeding had taken place. The program began in 1966 when the Pentagon's top R&D office, that of the Director of Defense Research and Engineering, proposed using cloud-seeding techniques in Southeast Asia as a means of inhibiting the movement of enemy troops and supplies. There followed a series of experimental tests in the Laos panhandle in October 1966. Authorized by Secretary of Defense McNamara, the tests were conducted by technical personnel from the Naval Weapons Center. This laboratory, located in China Lake, California, had been developing weather-modification technologies for several years. Fifty-six cloud-seedings were conducted, and over 85 percent of the clouds reacted favorably. In November 1966, on the basis of these tests, Col. Ulysses S. Grant Sharp, Jr., then commander in chief of the United States Pacific Fleet, concluded that "rainmaking" could be used as a valuable tactical weapon. Higher civilian Pentagon authorities were informed and consented to an operational program.

6. Details of the seeding program and decision-making process can be found in formerly secret testimony made public in the U.S. Congress, Senate Committee on Foreign Relations, Subcommittee on Oceans and International Environment, 93rd Congress, 2nd Session, *Hearings, Weather Modification* (Washington, D.C.: USGPO, 1974), pp. 87–123.

The Pentagon Papers explains that "various separate proposals" for ways of expanding the air war were made by the
Joint Chiefs of Staff (JCS) in December 1966 and January
1967. In February 1967 these were incorporated in a single
memo that JCS sent to President Lyndon B. Johnson. It said:
"Laos Operations . . . Authorization required to implement
operational phase of weather modification process previously
successfully tested and evaluated in the area." The operational phase of the program began in March 1967. As Deborah Shapley notes, "It appears then, that some approval at the
Presidential level" was made that moved the program into
Operations" in February or March 1967."[7] Thus, from 1967
to 1972, covert "operational seeding" took place in an attempt to slow the movement of the North Vietnamese troops
and supplies through the Ho Chi Minh Trail network.[8] Only
a few individuals in the White House and Congress knew
about the program. Among other non-DOD officials who were
aware of the program were: the Secretary of State and a limited supporting staff (including the Undersecretary for Political Affairs); the Director of the Central Intelligence Agency
and a limited supporting staff; and the chairmen of the House
and Senate Appropriations and Armed Services Committees.
The Thai government was not aware of the program, and the
Laotian government was only told that a general interdiction
campaign was being waged. No one at the Arms Control and
Disarmament Agency was informed. Apparently, those with a
"need to know" did not include those likely to oppose the
move.

How well the seeding "worked" could not be determined,
for there was a great deal of *natural* rainfall. However, there
were extremely severe floods in North Vietnam in 1971,
which caused widespread civilian suffering. Were they in any

7. *The Pentagon Papers*, Gravel Edition (Boston: Beacon Press, 1971), pp.
420–24. Cited in Deborah Shapley, "Weather Warfare—Pentagon Concedes
Seven-Year Vietnam Effort," *Science*, Vol. 184, June 7, 1974, p. 1060.
   8. Seymour M. Hersh, "U.S. Admits Rain-Making, 1967–1972, in Indochina,"
New York Times, May 19, 1974, p. 1:7.

way related to the seeding? The military said "No"; others merely speculated.

The technology may have worked to interdict enemy troops; it may also have had the effect of causing floods injurious to civilians; or it may not have mattered much at all, in view of the natural rainfall. The effectiveness is not at issue here. What is at issue is the fact that it occurred at all. It illustrates how easily new, uncertain, and possibly destructive technologies can be introduced into the military arsenal when the political estate and higher administrators are too busy to raise questions, when they look the other way, or may be regarded by those in control of the technology as not having a "need to know."

FEDERATED POWER AND SPACE APPLICATIONS

While there are rivalries and jurisdictional conflicts between developers and users even in a concentrated administrative system, these are usually minor compared with those in federated arrangements. In a federated system, more distinctive entities, with often quite disparate goals, are included. In a simple transfer between one government agency and another, more than the agencies are involved. Concerned also are the respective congressional committees and interest-group clienteles. In the concentrated system of DOD, the operational interests of the military estate tend to dominate the R&D biases of the technologists. In the federated pattern, where wholly separate organizations are concerned, the technoscience organization may be more powerful than the user. Moreover, the role of the Secretary of Defense provides leverage to resolve disputes within DOD's concentrated system. In the federated system, disputes may have to go one step higher to the Executive Office of the President.

From a national policy perspective, there is little question that there is a public interest in deploying space technology to practical uses on earth as quickly as possible. Within NASA, however, earth applications have traditionally had a status inferior to that of manned space flight and space science. The latter programs fall directly into the purview of what NASA has regarded as its primary mission: the exploration of outer space. Moreover, earth applications lie, at least partially, in the realm of agencies other than NASA. Since the termination of R&D on an applications program may mean the end of NASA's control over the program, NASA is understandably hesitant to move a technology to operations until it deems the technology "ready." It seeks to get the most possible political credit for the program before transferring it. A user, on the other hand, may have different ideas as to the readiness question. Frequently, the decision on readiness depends less on technical judgment than on bureaucratic power.

NASA AND THE WEATHER BUREAU

The case of NASA and the Weather Bureau was one of a strong technoscience agency and a weak user. At issue was the Tiros weather satellite, demonstrated in 1960. This was one of the first "practical" outputs of early federal activity in space. As the agency in charge of civilian space R&D, NASA regarded Tiros as but the first primitive step in weather satellite development. It went immediately to the creation of an advanced meterology satellite, Nimbus. The Weather Bureau, a potential user agency, had another point of view. It liked Tiros. Even this initial weather satellite could markedly improve its services.

To bring Tiros to operational capacity would require NASA to divert funds and manpower from *its* weather satellite development program to one that the space agency found relatively dull and unchallenging. The Weather Bureau, on its own, could not alter NASA's priorities. It found it had little choice but to contribute money to the design of the Nimbus development program, as the price of gaining some control over a satellite intended eventually for the Weather Bureau. There was no question that Nimbus would be technically better than Tiros. Eventually, Nimbus did succeed Tiros. In the early 1960's, however, the Weather Bureau had no desire to wait for the second-generation system when a first-generation satellite could be developed and placed in operation with relative ease. Here was the classic problem of the user. It saw a solution to an immediate problem, that of delivering weather forecasts. But the solution was controlled by another agency. Worse, the other agency implied that it, rather than the customer, knew best.

The Weather Bureau sought to tilt the scale of bureaucratic influence to its side through allies. Under the aggressive leadership of the Assistant Secretary of Commerce for Science and Technology, Herbert Hollomon, the Weather Bureau worked primarily within the executive branch. (Its congressional support was slight, compared with that given NASA by the space committees.) Its most important ally was the Department of Defense. DOD was a user as well as a developer of space hardware. The Weather Bureau made it plain to NASA that it could go elsewhere if NASA did not satisfy its needs immediately. The Bureau of the Budget and the Office of Science and Technology sided with the Weather Bureau. To underline its own point, the Weather Bureau withdrew from the joint Nimbus development program in 1963. NASA now had an applications program with no user at the end. It knew that the program would, under those circumstances, have difficulty with the Bureau of the Budget. Consequently, in 1964, NASA surrendered. A formal agreement was signed between the developer and user in which it was made clear that the Weather Bureau would no longer be a junior partner in the meteorological space satellite program. Following the agreement, emphasis in NASA changed to Tiros, and an operational weather satellite was deployed in 1966.[9]

9. For a detailed account of the NASA/Weather Bureau dispute, see Richard Chapman, *TIROS-NIMBUS: Administrative, Political, and Technological Problems of Developing U.S. Weather Satellites* (Syracuse, N.Y.: Interuniversity Case Program, Inc., 1972).

NASA AND THE INTERIOR DEPARTMENT

The pull of the Weather Bureau, thanks to its allies, was sufficient to move Tiros into operations and out of the control of NASA. The Interior Department, not long thereafter, engaged NASA in a similar contest in respect to Landsat, then known as the Earth Resources Technology Satellite (ERTS).

Landsat is a highly sophisticated, satellite-borne camera in space, capable of taking photographs and sensing the planetary resources with remarkable resolution. An experimental Landsat was launched by NASA in 1972. Its origins go back to 1964. Critics complain that the pace of Landsat has been much too "leisurely"[10] Why so leisurely a pace? The answer is that both the development push *and* demand pull were weak. For Stuart Udall, Secretary of the Interior during the Kennedy and Johnson administrations, the matter of NASA's lack of push was central. "It was the blindness and foot-dragging of NASA that started the delays," Udall has charged. "As far back as 1965, I tried to get the NASA people interested, and even tried to butter-up [NASA administrator] Jim Webb. I told the NASA people, 'After you reach the moon, interest is going to wane, and people are going to start asking what you have done for them lately.' I thought an earth applications program was a perfect means of bringing the benefits of space back to earth."

Udall offered to contribute to the deployment of an operational satellite, but Webb refused.[11] Webb, no doubt, did not disagree as to the utility of Landsat. He merely wished to make sure that when those benefits were brought back to earth some would fall to NASA. This was an unlikely prospect, from NASA's perspective, if the public identified Landsat prematurely as an Interior Department satellite. Hence,

10. For a more detailed account of this decision-making process, see W. Henry Lambright, "ERTS: Notes on a Leisurely Technology," *Public Science,* August/September 1973.
11. Richard D. Lyons, "Satellite-Borne Dowsing Rod To Be Orbited in Spring," *New York Times,* February 4, 1972, c,11:2.

Webb resisted the pull of the Interior Department, and Udall did not have the power to overcome that resistance.

In part, the weakness of the Department of Interior lay in the fact that it had opposition from other potential users. The Weather Bureau, as *the* civilian user of weather satellites, did not have rivals. The Interior Department did—in the Department of Agriculture and the Weather Bureau's successor, the National Oceanic and Atmospheric Administration. Indeed, even NASA eyed the possibility of becoming the user of its own Landsat development. Consequently, there were many who had stakes in avoiding decisions of operational control, at least to the extent that the Interior Department might be the primary instrument for use. Moreover, the Weather Bureau operated in an environment in which the national administration was anxious to demonstrate pre-eminence in space as quickly as possible. Thus, there was topside leverage to deploy Tiros. National administrations, in the late 1960's and early 1970's, were interested primarily in keeping governmental costs down and avoiding decisions that were not urgent. Both objectives favored keeping Landsat a leisurely and experimental technology.

NASA AND THE COMSAT CORPORATION

In 1959, NASA capped its initial work in communications satellites with the launching of its first such satellite, Echo. In 1974, with the launching of ATS-F, NASA stated it would begin to terminate large-scale developmental efforts in this field. Between these two events, a new industry had been brought into being, with NASA having played a major policy as well as a technological role in that process. Indeed, it was a *change* in NASA policy that helped to open the way for the creation of the Comsat Corporation. The creation of this corporation helped to keep NASA in the communications satellite business perhaps longer than would have been the case had the *initial* NASA policy been carried out.

The initial NASA position was the policy of NASA's "political estate," not that of its career technocrats. The Eisenhower administration's appointee as NASA administrator was T. Keith Glennan, who took a stand that many of his subordinates questioned, namely, communications satellites should be deployed to private enterprise as soon as possible. He had faith that the market, as regulated by the Federal Communications Commission (FCC), would protect the public interest in the new technology.

To carry out this policy, however, it was necessary to demonstrate not only that the technology was ripe, but also that the private sector was ready to take the initiative. The world's largest corporation, American Telephone and Telegraph (AT&T), eagerly sought to demonstrate its competence. It volunteered to pay the government to launch *its* communications satellite system, Telstar. With Glennan pushing hard and President Eisenhower backing this pro-business thrust, as his last legacy to the incoming Democrats, NASA and the FCC set the machinery in motion for the Telstar launch.

The Kennedy administration placed in office its NASA administrator, James Webb. Webb immediately saw not only organization interest in preventing a *fait accompli* by AT&T, but also a national policy need to review the Eisenhower/Glennan/FCC stance on communications satellite ownership. To buy time for NASA and the Kennedy administration, Webb substituted NASA R&D funds for AT&T money in the Telstar launch and let contracts to other corporations for the development and launch of systems alternative to Telstar. Thus, the government kept open technical and policy options that might have been foreclosed had the original NASA policy proceeded according to plan.

Afterward, one of the 1960's great debates involving new technology ensued.[12] There was much posturing on both sides, with cries of "monopoly," "big business," and the "vir-

12. For an account of the Glennan policy and the Communications Satellite Act of 1962, see Roger A. Kvam, "Comsat: The Inevitable Anomaly," in Sanford A. Lakoff, ed., *Knowledge and Power* (New York: The Free Press, 1966), pp. 271–92.

tues of private enterprise." There was even an unusual liberal filibuster in the Senate, on the part of those who stood for public ownership, against a "giveaway" to the private sector. As a consequence, the Eisenhower "legacy" did not stand unchanged. What resulted from the Communications Satellite Act of 1962 was the Communications Satellite Corporation (Comsat), a hybrid organization: quasi-private, quasi-public. Since much of the debate involved AT&T, Comsat might well be viewed as a national decision to prevent the possibility of AT&T's dominating the new technology. Had not the government specifically intervened as it did, AT&T's enormous economic position might have been extended to outer space.

The significance of displacing AT&T was not just ideological/economic. There were technological alternatives to Telstar. Comsat was new and open to purchasing whatever technological system might best serve its operational interests. The existence of *this* user kept NASA in the communications satellite business and permitted the development and deployment of the "ultimate" communications satellite—the Synchronous Communications Satellite (Syncom). Developed by NASA and the Hughes Aircraft Corporation, Syncom was judged operational in 1965 and was deployed to Comsat. AT&T had earlier been skeptical of the potentialities of a synchronous satellite: a satellite that moved synchronously with the earth's rotation, 22,300 miles in space. But Hughes had believed in the technology and had the support of advocates within NASA. Once demonstrated, Syncom was the user's choice.[13]

13. The synchronous orbit has been called by one NASA official "the most important place we have discovered yet in our advance into space." As the *New York Times* has noted: "At 22,300 miles above the Equator, a satellite travels at precisely the speed the earth is turning. Three satellites so placed around the Equator, passing messages back and forth, can maintain constant communications between any two points on earth." Quote from "Some New World Business: Rent-a-Satellite," *New York Times,* February 2, 1974, e,7:1. In contrast to Syncom, the AT&T Telstar system would have, at least initially, required 25 to 30 satellites in a low random orbit. There would have been coverage to the United States and Europe, and, at stated times, links with other locations. Kvam, *loc. cit.,* p. 280.

It is noteworthy that NASA's involvement in communications satellites continued beyond the first Syncom. The space agency began working on various advanced types of syncoms. As Comsat evolved more into a business than a public corporation, questions increasingly began to be raised in the Bureau of the Budget and Congress as to why NASA was subsidizing the R&D of a large and growing company. To retain its role, NASA masked its communications satellite work behind an Advanced Technology Satellite (ATS) series. ATS-F, launched in 1974, was made the last of this series, however, by a decision of the Nixon administration. This decision might have come more than a decade earlier had the Glennan approach to deploying the technology become national policy. Because of the delaying action of his successor, Webb, it did not. As NASA controlled the technology, NASA was the base for influence in national policy on the part of both Glennan and Webb. The Webb policy of maintaining the NASA developmental role was more congenial to NASA's organizational interests, of course. It was so much so that NASA maintained that policy as long as it could (for years after its architect, Webb, had departed).[14]

FEDERATED POWER AND THE PEACEFUL ATOM

Deploying the peaceful atom is undoubtedly one of the most complex civilian technology tasks undertaken by the federal government to date. The nature of the technology

14. The Nixon decision may have ended developmental activity aimed at new government-funded satellites. But NASA would presumably maintain a modest research role in the field, one that could be used to re-enter developmental activity at a later date. Moreover, ATS-F, while the last *NASA* satellite, was not the final communications satellite development project in which NASA participated. In 1975 came a cooperative project with Canada, the Canadian Cooperative Applications Satellite (CAS-C). It is not easy to kill completely a program that a technoscience agency or powerful forces in its environment want. (See Chapter 5 of this book.) For details on the ATS-F and concerns by Congress and others about NASA's "phase-down" in the field, see U.S. Congress, Senate Committee on Aeronautical and Space Sciences, 93rd Congress, 2nd Session, *Hearings, NASA Authorization for Fiscal Year 1975* (Washington, D.C.: USGPO, 1974), especially pp. 667–84, 727–31.

makes the atom both a potential boon and a threat to mankind. Until 1974, control over deployment was relatively tight. Within government, a powerful technoscience agency, the Atomic Energy Commission, had both development and regulatory responsibilities. It was overseen by centralized congressional power: the Joint Committee on Atomic Energy (JCAE). Working closely together, AEC and JCAE governed the atom, with national policy largely a legitimation of subsystem-level decisions.[15] The two bodies did not have total sway over deployment, however. In 1954, with a Republican administration in power, the Atomic Energy Act was rewritten to permit exploitation of the peaceful atom by the private sector. What this meant in practice was that AEC remained a developer/regulator, and the nation's electric utility companies became primary civilian users.

The 1974 legislation weakened the government side of the atomic partnership by placing nuclear energy within a general energy agency and making the regulatory part independent of the development segment. The changes reflected the administrative consequence of a more ambivalent national policy toward civilian atomic energy. The atom was still a special technology to be promoted by public R&D policy. But there was a greater desire to *control* as well as stimulate the technology—to balance nuclear energy with other sources of energy as well as to conserve energy. The creation of a Nuclear Regulatory Commission and an attempt to provide longterm, non-nuclear options via the Energy Research and Development Administration (ERDA) were manifestations of this new policy. The 1954 policy might be characterized as one of relatively unfettered promotion of the peaceful atom. The 1974 changes made for a guarded promotion. In both the old and new structures the system for R&D implementation was federated. There was a strong, central development organization, and there were generally strong, easily identified, im-

15. See Harold Green and Alan Rosenthal, *Government of the Atom* (New York: Atherton, 1963).

mediate users with a capacity to implement technology they adopted. However, the bureaucratic power behind the government side was less encumbered before 1974 than after.

It is worth reviewing the twenty years of AEC experience in deploying the peaceful atom to the electric utilities. By 1974 the first generation of civilian power reactors, based primarily on the Light Water Reactor (LWR) design, was being utilized.[16] Its place was not large—42 operational power plants supplying but 6 percent of America's electricity[17]—but there were many new plants being built. Even more were being planned, and there was a general feeling among both friends and enemies of the atom that America's energy future would be strongly nuclear. The users, in other words, had begun adopting the new technology. The pace was not as swift as had once been predicted. Also, many nuclear plants were operating well below capacity for reasons of safety and reliability. Still, the technology was diffusing through the industry.

AEC could bear much of the credit or blame for the state of civilian nuclear power affairs. It had provided enormous momentum for the commercialization of nuclear power. Seldom, if ever, has a federal agency pushed harder on a private industry to innovate a new technology. Initially, AEC did so in the wake of a national mandate. It continued to do so even as the national policy climate changed. In the end, the AEC itself was changed.

AEC AND THE ELECTRIC UTILITIES

The political process can be either a facilitator of or a constraint on administrative policy. In 1954, AEC was helped by the political environment in which it initially had sought to deploy the civilian atom. There was a national consensus in favor of putting the atom to peaceful use. The national deci-

16. John F. Hogerton, "The Arrival of Nuclear Power," *Scientific American*, Vol. 218, February 1968.

17. Claude E. Barfield, "Energy Report/Congress Weighs Major Shift in Reactor Licensing Procedures," *National Journal*, May 4, 1974, p. 647.

sion of 1946 had been for *civilian* control of atomic energy, but virtually the only customer AEC had known for eight years had been the military. AEC may have wished to move to new markets. Now, clearly, the country *wanted* AEC to look to civilian users. In his "Atoms for Peace" speech before the United Nations in 1953, President Eisenhower had captured the popular mood:

. . . the United States pledges before you—and therefore, before the world—its determination to help solve the fearful atomic dilemma—to devote its entire heart and mind to find a way by which the miraculous inventiveness of man shall not be dedicated to his death, but consecrated to his life.[18]

The attitude seemed to be: here is a resource, a solution; it has been used only for military purposes; billions have been and perhaps will be spent on developing the atom because of national security needs; surely, this awesome power can be used for constructive purposes also. In the early 1950's there was a sense almost of national mission, and the decision to deploy the peaceful atom was as political a decision as was that to go to the moon. There were no pressing economic or scientific reasons for doing so. In opening up the atom for private enterprise in 1954, industry may have wanted an ideological victory, but it really did not want to use the atom immediately. It did not regard nuclear power as yet ripe, from the competitive, commercial cost-perspective. The reality that AEC had to overcome was the fact that the economic market, for which the atom had been freed, did not need (or want) the product that AEC and the nation were promoting. Industry wanted the symbol of private control without the reality of operational use, expense, and risk.

AEC was supposed to develop and regulate the technology. The Light Water Reactor, thanks to AEC and Navy invest-

18. "Address before the General Assembly of the United Nations on the Peaceful Uses of Atomic Energy," New York City, Dec. 8, 1953. Public Papers of the Presidents of the United States, Dwight D. Eisenhower, 1953. Wash., D.C.: U.S.G.P.O., 1960, p. 822.

ments, was the "readiest" of reactor designs.[19] It was promoted by AEC and key equipment manufacturers to the utilities.[20] But industry hesitated. Very few potential users requested licenses from AEC. The ground-breaking for the first
demonstration reactor, jointly sponsored by AEC and the Du-
quesne Light Company, took place at Shippingport, Pennsylvania, in 1954.[21] Apparently, industry wished to await the
results of Shippingport, but Shippingport would not be in
operation until 1957. Under pressure from the Joint Committee to show results quickly, AEC gave increasingly greater emphasis not only to developing the technology but also to marketing it. Regulation was placed on the back burner.

AEC had to exercise a variety of incentives to stimulate industry. Shippingport became the beginning of a number of
"demonstration reactors." In 1955 AEC initiated a cooperative program with industry: the Power Demonstration Reactor Program (PDRP). Later that year, apparently unsatisfied
with the results of industry's response, AEC began a "second
round" of PDRP. A third round came in 1957, and yet a
fourth in 1962. Each round differed somewhat from the
others, but all had the common aim of user "pump-priming."
The government incentives varied, but usually AEC included
R&D assistance and waivers on initial costs of certain expensive nuclear items, such as fuel.[22]

These were formative years for AEC. For the second half of

19. AEC's Milton Shaw later commented: "If Admiral Rickover hadn't been
so damned successful with the Naval Light Water Reactor Program, the AEC
might well have gone directly to the Breeder." Quoted in Claude E. Barfield,
"Science Report/Nuclear Establishment Wins Commitment To Speed Development of Breeder Reactor," *National Journal*, July 17, 1971, p. 1497.

20. The role of equipment manufacturers was that of ally to AEC in the
effort to promote the atom to the target-users—the electric utilities. Such companies as General Electric and Westinghouse gained experience in government-
sponsored R&D and then became suppliers for operational products procured
by military and civilian users.

21. Not insignificantly, the project team that managed this demonstration
was headed by Admiral Rickover. For an excellent account of the Shippingport Project, see Richard G. Hewlett and Francis Duncan, *Nuclear Navy, 1946–
1962* (Chicago: University of Chicago, 1974), Chapter 8.

22. John F. Hogerton, "The Arrival of Nuclear Power," *loc. cit.*, p. 25.

the 1950's it was caught between a Democrat-controlled JCAE and a Republican White House. The former wanted accelerated deployment; the latter to keep government from interfering too much in market decisions. Demonstrations permitted governmental stimulation, but stopped short of overt subsidies to commercial operations. Once a particular demonstration had proved a certain reactor concept, AEC tended to pull back, except for continuing safety research. This administrative approach was described as a "love 'em and leave 'em" policy by the first chairman of the Nuclear Regulatory Commission, William Anders. Anders also noted that, with the government emphasizing the developmental aspects of the program and industry more attuned to strictly operational technology, a great deal of important technological work in the middle "fell between stools" and made for operating problems later on.[23]

Where did the role of government end and that of industry begin? The answer to this question seemed to depend on the readiness of the technology for operations. Even AEC seemed ambivalent on the question of the readiness of civilian atomic power. The licenses that AEC provided to industry were developmental, not commercial. This was a general AEC policy, not just the policy for special "demonstrations." Such licenses may have solved certain problems in government/industry relationships by allowing government to provide industry with some help (although not enough, in the view of Anders) while saving industry some legal problems.[24] As the technology diffused, the tendency to continue to give development licenses year after year raised a question in the minds of some observers: actually, how sure was AEC as to the atom's ripeness for routine use? In 1969 Richard Curtis and Elizabeth Hogan pointed out in *Perils of the Peaceful Atom* that "the

23. Remarks by William A. Anders at the Annual Conference of the Atomic Industrial Forum, Washington, D.C., October 31, 1974. Cited in *AEC News Releases* for the week ending November 13, 1974.

24. See Dorothy Nelkin, *Nuclear Power and Its Critics* (Ithaca, N.Y.: Cornell University Press, 1971), pp. 14, 15, 110–16.

nuclear power plant going up outside your community is officially an experiment."[25]

Readiness, which had been an issue for industry in the 1950's, became a general public question in the late 1960's. In the 1950's the users were as worried about nuclear accidents as nuclear critics were to be a decade later. They complained to AEC about the problem of getting private insurance. In the 1957 Price-Anderson Act, industry was assured of government indemnification. The Act set a limit of $560 million of indemnity on any radiological accident, but only $60 million of that amount would be put up by private operators. Thus did AEC/JCAE try to provide yet another positive incentive to industry.

However, AEC had sticks as well as carrots to apply to the users. As the president of one company remarked, "We acted to guarantee the position of private industry. The money spent was a gamble to preserve the private sector." Another president stated:

We made a proposal for what became Shippingport, and we breathed a good deal easier when we didn't get the contract. We weren't anxious to get into nuclear power, and I don't think any other company in its right mind wanted to get into it either. But you see, we had to bid—we had to act—whether we wanted to or not. We had been pushing the private development of nuclear power, and we couldn't refuse to get into it after pushing so hard.[26]

The political balance on the Joint Committee gave credibility to the public-power threat. In 1956 Senator Albert Gore and Representative Chet Holifield introduced a bill mandating AEC to construct six large-scale reactors in various

25. Richard Curtis and Elizabeth Hogan, *Perils of the Peaceful Atom* (New York: Ballantine, 1969), p. 242.

26. Cited in James W. Kuhn, *Scientific and Managerial Manpower in Nuclear Industry* (New York and London: Columbia University Press, 1966), p. 115.

parts of the country at a total cost of $400 million. The Gore-Holifield bill did not become law, but it made its point with AEC and the industry. In 1957 Louis Strauss, chairman of AEC, stated the choices before industry: "It is the Commission's policy," he declared, "to give industry the first opportunity to undertake the construction of power reactors. However, if industry does not, within a reasonable period of time, undertake to build types of reactors which are considered promising, the Commission will take steps to build the reactors on its own initiative."[27]

The adoption of nuclear power by the electric utilities was undoubtedly speeded by the AEC push. By the mid-1960's the arrival of nuclear power was proclaimed. John Hogerton saw the breakthrough as occurring between 1963 and 1966.[28] The new reactors going up and being ordered made it appear that the industry was regarding the atom as the wave of the future. This had a bandwagon effect. For the first time truly large-scale nuclear plants were being started. AEC's work was paying dividends at long last. No doubt it was aided by the financial and pollution problems suffered by the atom's fossil-fuel competition. From the user's perspective, the atom now looked like a commercially competitive technology.

In retrospect, the "success" of AEC by 1966 might have signaled that the time had come for the agency to promote less and to regulate more. Control of the technology might be said to have shifted to industry. In that event the development/marketing role of government could have receded as the regulatory role enlarged, but AEC was more a techno-science agency than regulator. It had worked too long and too hard creating a federated system based on government/industry partnership to begin thinking of the users as adversaries. Deployment, it could be argued, had a long way to go.

27. Philip Mullenbach, *Civilian Nuclear Power* (New York: Twentieth Century Fund, 1963), p. 10. Cited by Kuhn, *op. cit.*, p. 115.
28. Hogerton, *loc. cit.*, p. 26.

Government may no longer have dominated the implementation system as it had, but it was still needed as a strong partner. The Joint Committee, which was as promotion-minded as AEC, protected the Commission from critics in Congress. In the process, it may have insulated the agency from necessary political pressures for change.

In the late 1960's, the environmental movement and anti-technological trends fixed on the civilian atom. AEC seemed defensive, secretive, and suppressive of questions which some of its own technical personnel were raising about the readiness of nuclear energy. The nuclear critics grew in number and stridency. The technological partnership among AEC, industry, and JCAE became a tight and closed political subsystem. When the coalition ignored the call of the National Environmental Policy Act (NEPA) for environmental impact statements, it went too far, and the courts intervened.

The key case was Calvert Cliffs, decided in 1971. Judge J. Skelly Wright, speaking for the U.S. Court of Appeals of the District of Columbia Circuit, found that the agency's regulations violated the mandate of NEPA. The act had imposed "a substantive duty upon every federal agency to consider the effects of each decision upon the environment and to use all practicable means . . . to avoid environmental degradation."

Wright ordered AEC to reconsider all the licensing decisions made since NEPA had been passed. AEC was reminded that it had a "duty to see that important legislative purposes, held in the halls of Congress, are not lost or misdirected in the vast hallways of the federal bureaucracy."[29]

Shortly thereafter, James Schlesinger, the new AEC chairman, decided that AEC would not contest the ruling. In an address before a gathering of atomic industry, he declared, "You should not expect the AEC to fight the industry's politi-

---

29. Cited in Richard S. Lewis, *The Nuclear Power Rebellion: Citizens v. The Atomic Industrial Establishment* (New York: Viking Press, 1972), p. 282. The court case is *Calvert Cliffs Coordinating Committee v. AEC*. United States Court of Appeals, District of Columbia Circuit, July 23, 1971 (No. 42839 and No. 24871).

cal, social, and commercial battles. The AEC exists to serve the public interest."[30]

AEC had *thought* it was serving the public interest all along by promoting the peaceful atom in alliance with industry. Maybe it was—in the 1950's and early 1960's. During that period administrative and national policy were moving in tandem. Later, national policy shifted, while AEC conducted business as usual. By the end of the decade many regarded the atom more as a threat than a hope. The 1974 legislation merely wrote into administrative action what was the new national mood. Under the changes, the atom's bureaucratic power was curtailed; the regulatory arm was made independent of the promotional wing; and, the development side of AEC was placed under a general energy administrator and in direct competition with greatly strengthened, nonnuclear technoscience organizations. The government was still pushing the atom, but with an ambivalence born of fear.[31]

CONCLUSION

Who governs the pace and direction of high technology deployment? High technology is more than advanced or science-based technology. In the military, space, and atomic contexts, it is government-based technology. The agencies that sponsor the launching of technology influence the deployment of their creations. How much they influence that deployment depends on their leverage over users. How they use that leverage depends on administrative policy. Administrative policy

30. Cited by John Holdren and Philip Herrera, *Energy* (San Francisco and New York: Sierra Club, 1971), p. 190.

31. Speaking of the dangers of accidents, transportation, and waste disposal implicit in the full-scale deployment of nuclear energy, particularly that using the breeder reactor, Alvin Weinberg, former director of AEC's Oak Ridge National Laboratory, has written: "We nuclear people have made a Faustian bargain with society . . . the price that we demand of society for this magical energy source is both a vigilance and a longevity of our social institutions that we are quite unaccustomed to." "Social Institutions and Nuclear Energy," *Science,* Vol. 177, July 7, 1972, p. 33.

is a consequence of influences, internal and external, upon technoscience agencies.

In the concentrated administrative-technological system of DOD, where the agency is the customer of its own sponsored technology, the pace of deployment tends to be most influenced by the military users. The users are active early in the weapons innovation process. For DOD developers to get a project started and maintained requires user support. DOD developers and users are partners, with developers dominant at the outset, but users gaining control as the technology moves along the R&D continuum. The demands of users tend to be key in DOD deployment policy, with that policy facilitated or constrained by the Secretary of Defense and outside political forces.

NASA is both a concentrated system and part of a federated arrangement. In manned space flight, the interests of NASA as developer and user are mutually reinforcing. But where NASA is merely the developer and another organization is the user, the interests of NASA may conflict with those of the user. The user may want deployment to it to move at a faster pace than NASA may prefer. Whether a user can enforce such a view depends on its power vis-à-vis the developer. In space applications to weather, earth resources, and communications, NASA has deliberately "held" technology in R&D. Such an administrative policy may or may not be in the public interest. A great deal depends on *who* is the user. Had NASA not maintained communications satellites in R&D in the way that it did, the Communications Satellite Act of 1962 might not have been possible. There might have been a *fait accompli* in the interest of AT&T. Moreover, by retaining control of the technology, NASA helped produce the synchronous-satellite breakthrough that made communications satellites the commercial success they have become.

In the case of AEC and civilian nuclear power, the technoscience agency did not contain developers and users, but developers and regulators. The users, the electric utilities, were outside the agency. Unlike the NASA experiences discussed, where industry and other agencies sought eagerly to use new space technology, AEC had to "induce" user interest in nuclear reactors. Because AEC had to promote so much, it regulated relatively little. The developers and marketers, not the regulators, governed AEC. This was not due to the inherent power of the scientific/technological estates within AEC. Technologists were in charge because they had as their allies the politicians on the Joint Committee.

What concentrated and federated administrative systems have in common is the strong role of technoscience agencies over the implementation process. That power is not absolute, as NASA discovered in its contest with the Weather Bureau concerning the meteorological satellites, but it is sufficient to provide such agencies with great influence in determining when technologies are deployed and by whom. The importance of such leverage can be appreciated by comparing what happens (or what fails to happen) in those governmental sectors where such administrative power is absent.

4

Introducing Socio-Technology

"IF WE CAN go to the moon, why can't we . . . ?" So goes the refrain. It is one of the ironies and shames of American public policy that so much can be done in one area of governance and so little in others related so concretely to day-to-day life in our festering cities and conurbations. An easy answer to the question phrased above is that the problems of metropolitan America are not technological, but social. While true in a sense, it belies the degree to which many domestic/social problems have technological components. Practically every public service function on which the city spends funds has an aspect involving hardware. Narrow or broad, the technological base is there, and it is subject to manipulation, improvement, and innovation.

The argument against technological change is similar to that used by the automobile industry in opposing safety devices on cars by claiming that the problem is the driver and not the technology. Human nature may be at the root of most accidents—but if better equipment can be given to the driver, it may yet save his life. One can wait for the millennium when the roots of poverty, crime, and a host of other social ills are extirpated. In the meantime, problems worsen. To the extent that technology can provide a measure of amelioration, it would seem advisable that it be used. Why is it not applied?

Or why is it applied so inappropriately or clumsily as to lend credence to the arguments of its critics?

The answer obviously lies not in technology *per se*. Most technologies pertaining to social problems are middle-level or low in terms of science-base or general sophistication. Very little R&D tends to be involved. There is more integration of existing technologies than creation of new technology. The R&D budgets of most of the agencies concerned with urban-oriented problems reflect this fact in the considerable sums devoted to demonstration projects. Such projects lie in the gray area of R&D and operations and are intended as much to market that which is known as to test and evaluate new systems.

When one asks the administrator in Housing and Urban Development (HUD), the Department of Transportation (DOT), or the Environmental Protection Agency (EPA) why better technology is not introduced to housing, transportation, or pollution control, the answer is invariably "the institutional constraints." Institutional constraints are often used as a euphemism for politics—the democratic politics that provide access for a variety of groups capable of erecting roadblocks to new urban technologies. Sayles and Chandler speak of the administration of federal R&D in terms of "political-business" systems.[1] Public administration is seen as involving a combination of strictly managerial and purely political concerns. There is a great deal more "politics" in the management of defense, space, and atomic energy than is often realized. There is even more in domestic/social agencies. There is certainly more political participation in the programs of these agencies. For the domestic/social agencies, the political environment pervades "technical/business" decision-making to an extreme degree. Such agencies may be called "socio-technological" to emphasize both their social goals and the fact that the constraints on their applications are more socio-

---

1. Leonard Sayles and Margaret Chandler, *Managing Large Systems: Organizations for the Future* (New York: Harper and Row, 1971), p. 320.

political than technical. For the high-technology agencies (at least, for DOD, NASA, and ERDA's atomic branch), a combination of expertise and/or constituency tends to provide administrative resources for achieving technological change. For the socio-technology agencies, such as HUD, DOT, EPA, etc., there is a distinct lack of power.

Sayles and Chandler speak of the administration of technological change in terms of "pressure" systems. The contrast between the high-technology and socio-technology agencies is striking in terms of their leverage on the operating systems that they seek to alter. If the strength of the administrative push on technology creates problems for democracy where certain agencies are concerned, its *lack* of push may be equally a problem in the realm of other organizations. "If it can be done, it will be done." Although this is the message of the technological imperative, many technologies are *not* applied to domestic/social goals. The imperative appears to cut a selective swath across the federal bureaucracy.

The administrative systems for technological application discussed in the previous chapter were identified as "concentrated" and "federated." "Fragmented" aptly describes the administration of socio-technologies. The fragmentation of control over the applications process begins at the national level and extends to the cities. It is most apparent in the nature of the "user" of socio-technologies.

DOD develops technology for its own use. NASA does also, and when it develops technology for another entity, it usually has an influential relationship with that organization in determining how and when use occurs. AEC and its successor agency, ERDA, have developed atomic technology for military and industrial users that are easily identifiable if not always controllable. The socio-technology agency, however, in its role as a development organization, often has difficulty even identifying the user of its products. The "market" is hardly the agency itself, but rather state and local governments or a private industry fractionated in hundreds and sometimes thousands of ways. As Sayles and Chandler state:

The Department of Housing and Urban Development does not control housing. It encounters vested interests wherever it turns. An environmental-control agency will have complex relationships with industry, which will be a contractor, a user, and an element the agency is regulating. Missions in housing and environmental protection also have the flavor of construction and maintenance efforts, involving continuous upgrading and improvement. Many of the programs will have to deal with political complexities NASA never dreamed of—interfaces that are more readily identified than managed. Dramatic goals to mobilize public opinion and focus diverse professionals, such as landing on the moon, may be hard to come by. The day New York City gets fresh air may be of great significance to man on earth, but it does not have the same impact.[2]

Who speaks for the user? That is a question socio-technology administrators constantly confront. In the domestic/social sphere, authority is splintered, not only between levels of government and between public and private sectors, but also between management and labor. Union power is a monumental factor in decisions to use new technology in most of the public service areas of the city. A transportation union may say "No" to a new mass transit system. By no means does management always prevail in such a conflict. Indeed, in anticipation of trouble, management may shy away from decisions to introduce new technology. Why take risks?

Finally, in socio-technology, there is a proximity between the user and the public that is not present in the high-technology fields. Protests over nuclear reactors notwithstanding, user decisions in high technology tend to be treated as authoritative by most affected citizens. The patient seldom questions the judgment of the doctor who prescribes a new

2. *Ibid.* See Chapter 15 of Sayles and Chandler on "socio-technical" systems.

drug. The patient may well be the *ultimate* user of the new technology, but the authoritative decision on use lies with the doctor. So it is with military, space, and atomic applications. The public is, at least indirectly, an ultimate user, customer, or beneficiary of all these technologies. Nevertheless, the immediate user, the organization concerned with delivery of such technologies, tends to make the controlling decisions. When the user "adopts," it can generally also "implement." In contrast, people do involve themselves more in both phases of "use" decisions when it comes to domestic/social technologies, for they are not so much awed by the expertise of the "professional." They *know* something about whether they find a house attractive or a transportation system convenient. By refusing to buy a house or to use a mass transit system, they affect the decisions of the private or public organization that, from a technoscience agency's perspective, is the user. In socio-technology, the public's reach over use decisions is longer. Once a nuclear power plant is operating the public will use it; electricity is needed regardless of the source. On the other hand, an operating urban mass transit system may be ignored in favor of the car. For better and worse, socio-technologies are thus more citizen-participatory.

The greater integration of developers/users in high technology, whatever the conflicts between them, helps explain the relative swiftness of application. Where relationships between the necessary actors are distant, hard to identify, or difficult to establish, there is far more opportunity for failure in communication and for working at cross purposes. The underdevelopment of routinized relationships within an administrative system means frailty in the broader, political-policy process and leads to continuing low levels of budgetary support for domestic/social R&D.

High-technology agencies have escaped most of the fragmenting forces of federalism, unions, and citizen participation. The functional congressional committees overseeing such technoscience agencies have been promotionally inclined. The socio-technology agencies have operated in a much different environment. They are more "open," but also more divided; more democratic, but less efficient or effective in applying the fruits of R&D. Where many are in charge, often no one controls.[3] Technologies that might do some good may thus sit on the shelf indefinitely. If demonstrated, they may not be adopted. If adopted, users may still not be able to implement them.

The issues confronting a better integration of science and technology with the city can best be illustrated by focusing on two of the most important urban services: housing and mass transit.

FRAGMENTED POWER AND HOUSING

According to Harvey Brooks, "Technology seems to progress most successfully when it fills a vacuum and to encounter the greatest resistance when it tries to penetrate an existing technostructure. It is this factor which makes innovation in the civilian sector most difficult."[4] Viewed another way, Brooks is suggesting that it is harder to change an old industry than to initiate a new one. The housing or building-construction industry is an example of a "mature" industry, and it has certainly been difficult to alter its character.

Even AEC, with all its power, found it exceedingly slow to move the electric power industry into a nuclear future. The attitudes of the management of many firms had to be changed in order to displace the conventional technology. Federal housing agencies, with less power than AEC, have had to try to change an even more recalcitrant construction industry.

The building industry is huge, diffuse, and unwieldy. It is hard to even locate the boundaries of the industry. Depending upon what is included or excluded, its size is anywhere

3. As Harlan Cleveland has asked, "How Do You Get Everybody in on the Act and Still Get Some Action?" *Maxwell News and Notes* (Syracuse, N.Y.: Maxwell School, Syracuse University, Fall 1974), pp. 57–61.
4. Harvey Brooks, as cited by Dorothy Nelkin in *The Politics of Housing Innovation* (Ithaca, N.Y.: Cornell University Press, 1971), p. 84.

from fifty to eighty billion dollars a year.[5] Characterized by extreme compartmentalization, it includes some 85,000 general building contractors, 9800 architectural and engineering firms, as well as innumerable materials suppliers, realtors, entrepreneurs of building enterprises, and public and private financial backers.[6] A "private" enterprise, the building industry nevertheless is inextricably bound by public regulations at federal, state, and local levels. Such regulations, particularly the local building codes, have hamstrung technological change. Many have outlasted the purposes for which they were originally promulgated. This industry cannot be discussed without reference also to the construction unions of electricians, plumbers, etc., whose members tend to be highly skilled, highly paid, and highly conservative in terms of the conditions of their work.

How does innovation take place in so fragmented, regulated, and unionized an industry? The largest builder in the housing industry does not produce more than 1 or 2 percent of the total supply.[7] This makes a federal strategy for change difficult to formulate and even harder to implement. Where is leverage applied? Would it matter which companies were "early adopters" in such an industry? Technologies diffuse through imitation. Almost from necessity, the housing industry takes its cue, not from other "leading" firms across the country, but from the desires of specific home and building buyers at the local level. Such buyers tend to be even more conservative than builders. Innovation is fine—but not on *my* house. The orders tend to be small. The industry is tailored to the market. It is fragmented, cautious, and localized. Buildings are constructed on site. All the needed materials and

5. *Ibid.,* p. 6.
6. Donald A. Schon, *Technology and Change* (New York: Delta, 1967), p. 156.
7. U.S. Department of Housing and Urban Development, *Design and Development of Housing Systems for Operation Breakthrough* (Washington, D.C.: USGPO, n.d.), p. 3.

parts are brought together *there,* put together *there.* In bad weather, work is interrupted and delayed.

One of the most important segments of the economy, the building industry remains one of the most troubled. In 1963 an A. D. Little study found that "during the last thirty years, there has been no major technological change of major economic significance for the building industry. . . . Technological change has been primarily evolutionary in small increments, significant only in the aggregate. . . . It can hardly be called 'innovation'."[8]

Technological lag in an era of rising wages results in lower productivity.[9] For the person buying a home that means rising costs. In fact, the costs of housing have gone so high as to move beyond the pocketbooks of many citizens who would formerly have been potential homeowners. The boom in mobile homes in the United States is not entirely the result of personal choice. Often it is the consequence of economic necessity.

What should the federal government do? For years the federal government has helped to subsidize housing construction. In doing so it has largely paid for old technology, thus reinforcing the status quo. Efforts to use federal leverage to introduce more labor-saving and productive housing technologies have been episodic, and their fate demonstrates some of the complications of socio-technological application.

THE CIVILIAN INDUSTRIAL TECHNOLOGY PROGRAM

Dorothy Nelkin has described the first of two recent federal attempts to apply new technology to housing.[10] It was a sad story, at least for its would-be innovator, J. Herbert Hollomon, Assistant Secretary of Commerce for Science and Technology. He was successful in the struggle mentioned earlier to influ-

8. Nelkin, *Politics of Housing Innovation, op. cit.,* p. 7.
9. *Ibid.,* pp. 6–7.
10. *Ibid.*

ence the deployment of the Tiros weather satellite. In contrast, he was markedly *unsuccessful* in getting a housing R&D program launched as part of a broader Civilian Industrial Technology Program (CITP).

In 1962 Hollomon requested Congress to provide funds for a CITP with three prime aims: "to foster innovation in lagging industries, including building and textiles; to study the information needs and state of technology in other industries; and to create an industry-university service to diffuse information and provide technical aid." Hollomon wanted to transfer technology from space and defense to civilian industry. He was convinced that the technology was there, if only he could get civilian industries to think more innovatively. He did not believe "the market" was sufficient to stimulate change in lagging industries. Federal programs were needed, and his CITP was a good start, at least in Hollomon's view.

The CITP program was never fully funded and eventually died. Only that segment pertaining to textiles made any headway at all. The part that met the most opposition and thus epitomized the reaction to the whole was that concerning housing.[11] As the immediate users of the technology that Hollomon wished to transfer, the building industry had to support CITP if it were to succeed. Instead of support, Hollomon faced opposition.

The attitude of the building industry toward the program is revealed in the following statement by the Construction and Community Development Committee of the U.S. Chamber of Commerce:

The construction industry leaders of business firms and associations have not been asked if they want a centralization of responsibility for research and development vested in the federal government. . . . The Civilian Industrial Technology Program makes no contribution to the private enterprise system. The private enterprise system requires limited government. The Con-

11. *Ibid.,* p. 3.

struction Civilian Industrial Technology Program adds more government intervention and higher levels of federal spending at a time when less government intervention and lower levels of federal spending are most needed by the construction industry.[12]

The resistance of the construction industry was echoed by its supporters in Congress. Moreover, Hollomon made some extremely serious tactical errors in his personal relations with key legislators whose help he needed, thereby winning enemies rather than friends for his program. Finally, the Department of Commerce was not ideal as an organizational base for a housing innovation program. The voice of business in government, it listened to an angry industry that feared modernization by government. Hollomon had limited support within the department. With Tiros, he had had legitimacy; he had been fighting for the prerogatives of an existing department agency, the Weather Bureau. Starting a housing R&D program in the Commerce Department meant organizational innovation *within* the department as well as outside. The Civilian Industrial Technology Program, thus, had much against it. It did not survive very long, and the most important segment (that relating to housing) never really made any progress at all.

OPERATION BREAKTHROUGH

In contrast to CITP, Operation Breakthrough, a second major federal effort at housing innovation, moved well beyond a technological proposal to become one of the very few, large-scale, socio-technology efforts to reach the deployment stage. The key figures behind the program were George Romney, Secretary of the Department of Housing and Urban Development, and Harold Finger, Assistant Secretary for Research and Technology. They operated in a more congenial bureaucratic and political environment than had Hollomon. The Department of Housing and Urban Development (HUD)

12. Cited in James D. Carroll, "Science and the City: The Question of Authority," *Science*, Vol. 163, February 28, 1969, p. 908.

had been created in 1965 to give a stronger voice in the federal establishment to the nation's cities and their problems. In the Great Society years of the Johnson administration, the mood of Congress was open to housing initiatives, as reflected in 1968 legislation which called for ". . . the construction or rehabilitation of twenty-six million housing units, six million of these for low and moderate income families." This was to be done in a decade. There had been housing goals before. In 1949 Congress had pledged to provide "a decent home and suitable environment for every American family."[13] When Romney took office he vowed to fulfill the 1968 mandate.

Romney likened the housing objective to the lunar goal of Apollo. In Finger, he had a former NASA executive. Together, they were moving forces behind Operation Breakthrough, which was an attempt to accelerate the production of houses through a modularized, factory-built approach. As a former automobile executive, Romney had seen cars come off an assembly line. Why not houses? The more houses that could be produced, the lower the costs would be. HUD could meet its ten-year goal as NASA had met its goal.

With Romney's backing, Finger adopted a "scientific approach" to Breakthrough. There would be three phases in the program: (1) contracting for prototype builders and site location for particular breakthrough developments; (2) actually constructing, testing, and evaluating prototypes in factories and then moving them to their sites for public occupancy; and (3) volume production. Phases one and two would be government-sponsored. The third would be left largely to the market.

Breakthrough was to be a model socio-technology program. Finger designed a program with primary and secondary goals, or what some critics regarded as "overt and covert" goals. The primary goal was purely technological: building industrial-

13. U.S. Department of Housing and Urban Development, *Operation Breakthrough* (Washington, D.C.: USGPO, n.d.), p. 9.

ized houses. To achieve that goal meant "breaking through" the host of barriers to innovation in the construction industry. As Finger put it, Breakthrough was "an effort to improve the entire process of housing—including the methods by which we produce and provide that housing to all our people." To accomplish the goal "improvement in production, materials, performance criteria, design, land use, site planning, marketing, financing, community attitude, and overall management" was required.[14]

Breakthrough was thus to be a technological Trojan Horse. What might not be possible as direct social change might be feasible if linked, indirectly, to a hardware goal that Congress had already declared in the public interest. The social dimension of Breakthrough was evidenced in a number of ways. With respect to the attitude of the building industry, HUD sought to catalyze change by fostering the invasion of housing by aerospace companies. This inevitably was seen as a threat by conventional builders. It made some of the larger organizations take industrialized housing more seriously. With respect to unions, the effort at social change went beyond mere attitudes. The building crafts were notoriously under-representative of blacks and other minority groups. Industrialized, prefabricated housing could use many low-salaried, low-skilled workers, many of whom could be black. This would open construction work to formerly excluded citizens, while at the same time lowering labor costs. Then there was the problem of building codes. If these could be made more uniform across the country, materials could travel in interstate commerce and be produced in accord with *national* performance criteria. To a remarkable degree, negotiations between HUD and state housing officials paid off in getting more uniform codes. In fact, in four years, Operation Breakthrough produced the following record:

14. Harold Finger, "Operation Breakthrough: The Scientific Approach," *HUD Challenge*, March 1971, p. 12.

(1) Approximately 2800 housing units, using industrial assembly techniques and involving various innovative features, were fabricated and erected to demonstrate the quality, value, and potential of industrialized methods of housing production.

(2) Nine prototype sites in eight metropolitan areas were developed as showcases for this housing, to demonstrate what good site planning could do to improve the living environment.

(3) New forms of labor contracts were developed by the building trade unions and the new, manufactured housing industry provided for organization of the housing factory on an industrial union basis, with wages and work rules appropriate to factory work rather than field work. The training and employment of disadvantaged individuals and groups were thus deliberately and successfully encouraged.

(4) Approximately half of the states enacted statewide regulations permitting the use of factory-built housing in any community in the state, overcoming the traditional constraint of diverse and restrictive building codes and regulations. Several other states also had such legislation in process. None had enacted such laws prior to Breakthrough.[15]

Some goals were too controversial to be obscured by Breakthrough's hardware. Two sites for Breakthrough prototypes were cancelled, in part due to local pressure. Some white citizens saw Breakthrough as a vehicle for introducing new neighbors—blacks—along with new technology. Where the secondary goals, real or imagined, became an issue, Breakthrough was met with resistance, including antagonism in the congressional committees to which HUD reported. The original Breakthrough plans called for 3000 prototype units on 11

15. U.S. Department of Housing and Urban Development, *Operation Breakthrough, op. cit.*, pp. 4, 5.

sites in 10 states, but HUD suffered a budget cut for FY-1971. The HUD request of $55 million for R&D, most of which was aimed for Breakthrough, was reduced to $30 million.[16]

If Congress did not share the commitment of Romney and Finger to industrialized housing, neither did the Nixon administration. Wedded to a market-oriented ideology, it opposed most federal efforts to stimulate civilian sectors of the economy. The goal of 26 million new houses by 1978, inherited from President Johnson's years, seemed hardly sacrosanct. The various complaints about Breakthrough's secondary goals did not escape notice on the part of politicians in the White House.

In 1973, when Nixon began his second term, he chose not to reappoint Romney and Finger to their HUD positions. This was part of a general "housecleaning" of Nixon's first-term appointees, but it proved especially important for Breakthrough, for its champions were removed. HUD's new leaders presided over the transition of Breakthrough into phase three, where it would succeed or fail in accordance with market demand.

According to Kenneth Zapp:

HUD did have power to help create a demand for industrialized housing through various non-R&D demonstration programs. It could give priority in the allocation of housing assistance funds to proposals that planned to use Breakthrough systems. Communities that raised no objections to use of these systems for all income levels (and, implicitly, races) would be given priority in their funding requests to HUD for water and sewer facilities, community facilities, and urban renewal financing.[17]

In other words, HUD had the necessary policy instruments to aid Breakthrough even in phase three. What was needed was the political and administrative will to apply such tools to

16. Kenneth Zapp, "Industrialized Housing and Public Policy," *Technology Review*, February 1972, p. 23.
17. *Ibid.*, p. 25.

keep the momentum going for technological change. This was missing once Romney and Finger left. In 1974 a National Academy of Sciences panel evaluated the results of Breakthrough. It found: "None of the Operation Breakthrough objectives have been achieved nor is there evidence that what has been done in the program will act as a catalyst for eventual achievement." On the other hand, the panel said, "neither has the program proven that the objectives could not be reached, given different circumstances and sufficient time and money."[18]

Breakthrough was hardly a "solution" to the country's housing woes. As critic Ada Louise Huxtable argued, industrialized, assembly-line production of housing could not work within the established system. It would "require the total reorganization of the building industry into a coordinated, vertical, production-shipping-assembly format," which would be an "outrageously costly procedure." She contended that the premise that industrialization dealt with the main cost of housing was fallacious. She said, "The house unit itself—materials and labor—represents only half of the total costs; the onsite cost is less than one percent. Big chunks of housing costs are in land (23%) and money (25%), problems no one is solving."[19]

From the beginning, Breakthrough was oversold. This one program did not have the leverage to reform the construction industry or remove the institutional constraints surrounding innovation in housing. However, in view of its four-year accomplishment its record might have been more impressive and judgments of it less severe had it survived somewhat longer. Consider the contrast in political will between the backing of Breakthrough and that of civilian nuclear reactors. Breakthrough had only one "round" to sell the various users

18. National Academy of Sciences, National Research Council, Technical Panel of Advisory Committee to the Department of Housing and Urban Development, _A Report on Operation Breakthrough_ (Washington, D.C.: National Academy of Sciences, 1974), p. 75.

19. _HUD Challenge,_ June 1974, p. 1.

on industrialized housing. AEC had at least four, officially,[20] and the pressure and incentives applied to industry users, for nuclear application, have been endless. The National Academy of Sciences panel chastised HUD for not treating Breakthrough more as an "experiment."[21] As a "demonstration," it had to succeed. On the other hand, who would want to buy or live in an "experimental" modular home? As seen in housing, the political rules under which the game of innovation is played are quite different in the high-technology and the socio-technology arenas. In the latter, administrators apparently have a much shorter period in which to score all their points and are not permitted the luxury of "demonstrating" anything but success.

FRAGMENTED POWER AND URBAN MASS TRANSIT

The urban mass transit industry has been in deep financial trouble for many years. Even with federal subsidies, it has not thrived. As David Miller points out:

By virtually any measure, the urban mass transit industry has been in decline for at least 20 years. Employment, fleet size, and number of passengers carried have all fallen. Gross revenues have remained fairly stable in the recent past, but this is because fare increases have offset the decrease in ridership. Prospects for the industry generally are not bright, and private ownership is waning rapidly. Of the transit properties in our ten largest cities, only Houston's is still in private hands; many medium-size cities' transit firms have already 'gone public'; and mass transit has disappeared entirely in a large number of cities of less than 100,000 population.[22]

The recognition of mass transit as a "public good" has come only as a last-minute rescue operation. The public

20. John F. Hogerton, "The Arrival of Nuclear Power," *Scientific American*, February 1968, pp. 21–31.
21. National Academy of Sciences, *op. cit.*, p. 74.
22. David Miller, "Financing Mass Transit: Mobility Is Among the Assets," *Technology Review*, December 1973, p. 45.

money that is spent tends to be used to shore up old technology rather than to produce innovative transit systems that might entice automobile riders to use them. The replacement of private with public management has not resulted in more risk-taking leadership. It has not caused the transit unions to refrain from striking to get what they want, as well as to avoid innovations they do not want. It has seldom led to better service for the public. It has not even made for cooperation between federal, state, and local transit agencies. There is as much rivalry between the levels of government as between public and private sectors. The system of transportation-policy/administration is like that of housing: fragmented, directionless, cautious in implementing any change that might lose further customers. Rewards are few in public management, but penalties come swiftly. So why take risks? Why innovate?

The federal Urban Mass Transit Administration (UMTA) in the Department of Transportation (DOT) is hardly a show-case of risk-taking itself. Like HUD, of which it was once a part,[23] UMTA has been slow to evolve from a relatively passive, grant-giving agency, largely responding to the operational interests of states and cities. To do more is to go against the grain of the New Federalist philosophy that has taken hold in recent years. It has, therefore, been an exceedingly mild stimulus for innovation. Like the user constituency, UMTA's program has been conservative and disjointed. In the few instances that it has tried to update urban mass transit, it has run into enormous problems at all levels of government.

In its attempt to perform as a technoscience agency, UMTA's dilemma is to induce change both in private-sector manufacturers and public-sector (state and local government) users. The fact that part of the users in the fragmented system

23. UMTA was transferred following the creation of the Department of Transportation in 1966.

of UMTA are "public" does not necessarily ease the way for federally inspired technology. As with housing, the users of mass transit technology are dispersed, unionized, and influenced greatly by the sentiments of the ultimate customers—the riding public. Edward David, while serving as Nixon's science adviser, stated that the federal government and the cities and states would have to work together:

. . . to develop the system of transportation that will best serve the user. [He is speaking of "user" as the rider.] To get the cars out of the cities will require a system that is attractive to the user as well as some motivation to leave the cars out of the city. In accomplishing these goals, the federal government can be a resource in the design of new people-movers, but the state and local governments must have enough input to assure that the equipment available fits their needs. Further, to demonstrate the technical and economic feasibility of new transportation systems requires the intimate involvement of state and local governments working in close cooperation with federal R&D agencies.[24]

David thus suggests the formula for socio-technological application in the field of urban mass transit: the federal government to be a "resource in the design of new people-movers"; the state and local governments to have "enough input to assure that the equipment available fits their needs"; and "close cooperation" between the various governmental entities "to demonstrate the technical and economic feasibility." Here is cooperative federalism aimed at developing and delivering good transportation to the riding public. It is a classic formulation—so easy to say, so hard to consummate. Consider "cooperative federalism" as revealed when UMTA decided to demonstrate a new concept in bus transportation—Dial-A-Ride.

24. Address by Dr. Edward David, National Action Conference on Intergovernmental Science and Technology Policy, Harrisburg, Pennsylvania, June 21, 1972.

DIAL-A-RIDE

Dial-A-Ride (DAR)[25] was among the first tentative efforts of UMTA to innovate in urban mass transit technology in the United States. A DAR vehicle is a cross between a conventional bus and a taxi. It provides some of the convenience of taxi service with the low cost of buses. Its aim is to be "demand responsive," that is, to respond to the needs and wishes of the customer rather than to force the customer to meet the requirements of the technology. Only mass transit systems that provide some of the convenience of the automobile can hope to win back riders. Moreover, demand-responsive systems meet another need which is often overlooked—mobility for the poor, elderly, and handicapped who do not own cars. Such individuals have suffered as mass transit has declined in America.

To use a Dial-A-Ride bus, a customer merely telephones the central dispatcher and tells him the point of origin, the destination, and the number of passengers. The dispatcher assigns a vehicle to handle the request, either manually or with a computer, and tells the customer how long the wait will be. By radio he tells the driver of the assigned vehicle to make the pickup. The larger the area to be serviced, the more vehicles, etc., the more sophisticated and computerized is the system. The DAR is well within the state-of-the-art, and small-scale, manually operated systems were begun with local public or private initiative in a few cities in the United States and Canada before UMTA launched a national demonstration DAR project in Haddonfield, New Jersey (population: 12,961) in 1972. The roadblocks to getting this particular demonstration under way reveal why urban mass transit modernization comes so slowly.

25. Material in this section is based upon the author's "Innovating in Urban Mass Transit: The Case of Dial-A-Ride," unpublished manuscript (Syracuse, N.Y.: Maxwell School, Metropolitan Studies Program, Syracuse University, 1972).

A number of factors argued in favor of Haddonfield as a demonstration site: the socio-economic mix of the town was balanced; the opportunity the selection afforded to test DAR as a feeder for a high-speed line from Haddonfield, where people lived, to nearby Philadelphia, where they worked; and the general political support for mass transit (and UMTA) among the state's congressional delegation. The dominant reason, however, for placing the first national demonstration of DAR in Haddonfield related to federal UMTA's perception of the immediate user, the State Department of Transportation.

As noted, fragmentation of local control over transportation services is regarded as a key problem in federal attempts to stimulate socio-technological innovation. Many state DOT's must share power with a myriad of state and city agencies over transportation functions. New Jersey DOT was regarded by Washington authorities as unusually powerful and authoritative. UMTA could deal, therefore, with "one body" in working with New Jersey. If New Jersey DOT wanted to put a transportation demonstration in Haddonfield, it had the power to do so with a minimum of bureaucratic clearances. Furthermore, the commissioner of New Jersey DOT was the former administrator of UMTA and very much pro-DAR. Hence, the federals felt that they would have strong support at the state level in providing the best possible administrative environment for the DAR demonstration. UMTA felt that this particular user would be helpful to the *national* goals of the demonstration, rather than an obstacle to those goals.

The New Jersey proposal to run the DAR demonstration came to UMTA in August 1970. Ordinarily, it would have been funded automatically since most of the important agreements had been worked out informally prior to the actual submission of the proposal, but the federal Department of Labor (DOL) held up the grant award. The fragmented control which UMTA had sought to avoid at the state and local level had precipitated this first obstruction. DOL's move was a consequence of local problems. That DOL could stymie UMTA showed that power over mass transit is dispersed at the federal level as well as below.

Under the law, the Department of Labor had every right to hold up the award. The reason it could do so was the fact that New Jersey Senator Harrison Williams, a leading champion of public transit, was also a champion of "Big Labor." Labor had contributed $55,000 to his most recent election campaign. A landmark transit bill which he had helped draft in 1970 had substantially increased federal aid to urban mass transit. It also contained a clause (13C) that specifically protected transit employees against worsening their positions due to the use of more technologically advanced and productive hardware. At the time, what appeared to be an interagency dispute at the federal level was in reality a reflection of fragmentation at the local level. New Jersey DOT may have been in charge, bureaucratically, but it could not control the transit union.

The real dispute that delayed the DAR start-up was between New Jersey DOT and the state transit union. Although the issues pertained far more to matters in conventional transit than to the DAR demonstration, the union used DAR as one more "bargaining chip" in its negotiations with New Jersey. If the state wanted a Dial-A-Ride demonstration, it would have to accede on some other point labor wanted. The unions were able to reach into the Washington bureaucracy and place *their* agency against federal DOT, perhaps in the hope DOL would move federal DOT to press against New Jersey DOT.

As long as New Jersey and its transit unions bargained, federal DOL procrastinated, and UMTA could do little but wait. Eventually, in April 1971, the labor dispute was resolved, and New Jersey was officially awarded the grant to run the demonstration on behalf of UMTA. During the course of the long union dispute, however, other problems arose. New Jersey DOT had been chosen, as noted, because of its relative control over the transportation function in that state. What Washington had not expected was New Jersey's seeking to assert control over the Haddonfield demonstration. Who was in charge of the program? The project was conceived and funded by the federal government, but administered through a grant to the state. A demonstration project tends to fall somewhere between R&D and operations. What was the role of New Jersey DOT? It was certainly a user of an experimental system. Under the circumstances, was it also a co-developer? The lines of authority were blurred.

A serious intergovernmental dispute between UMTA and New Jersey came early. Like the union trouble, it delayed initiation of the actual project by several months. In designing the original specifications for the demonstration, UMTA had worked closely with a private contractor, Lex Dav. This company was generally seen as the logical choice to design and manage the experimental system for both the state and federal agencies. When the state made its proposal to UMTA, it used plans formulated, in large part, by Lex Dav. All seemed well until a middle-level, state DOT official blocked the award of a contract to Lex Dav. He put the project out on bids. This created additional delays and further threw the plans of federal UMTA askew. In the end, following some difficult negotiations and some political pressures as Boeing bid for the DAR contract, Lex Dav won the award. In August 1971, the state and the company agreed to a contract. Now the "real" preparations for the demonstration could be made.

In February 1972, one and one-half years after a presumably *pro forma* proposal from New Jersey went to UMTA, the first DAR buses rolled. As if to underline the fragility of the social environment in which the technology was proceeding, the state transit union struck again. When DAR service was resumed two months later, it continued its rather tortuous route, "demonstrating" quite well all of the reasons innovations come so slowly in urban mass transit.

The Dial-A-Ride introduction to New Jersey points up

some of the difficulties caused by "uncooperative federalism." But it says even more about the power of local interest groups in fragmented systems of administration. The most striking example of cooperation was that between the New Jersey unions and the U.S. Department of Labor. This axis was sufficient to offset whatever momentum UMTA and New Jersey DOT had generated behind the innovation. UMTA could not push very hard, with the Department of Labor standing in its path.

The Haddonfield case suggests that UMTA is a powerless agency. Actually, UMTA has a measure of potential leverage on the operating systems of urban mass transit. It can create new technology through R&D; it can then help to obtain demand through providing capital grants and other subsidies for the purchase and use of the same new technology. The power, however, has been largely latent. Where UMTA *did* exercise force to move a new technology, it did so for the wrong reasons under the worst of conditions. The Personal Rapid Transit (PRT) technology was demonstrated in Morgantown, West Virginia, on a "crash" basis, much to the chagrin of both R&D personnel and users connected with the project.

PERSONAL RAPID TRANSIT

The Personal Rapid Transit system represented quite a step forward from DAR in technology, money, and national visibility. It was a much higher priority project for many reasons, as will be noted. The goals in DAR were included in those of PRT: to get people out of their cars and into mass transit (to relieve congestion and pollution), and to aid the mobility of the elderly, handicapped, and poor. In the technological community, if not necessarily among mass transit users, there was genuine enthusiasm for PRT. Some held it was the one new system that could be run without a public subsidy. Many believed that it promised not only a solution for the country's urban transportation problems, but also a major new market for the aerospace industry.

PRT is akin to a horizontal elevator. Responding to a button pressed by a patron, small cars under remote control move around a fixed, perhaps elevated, guideway to pick up and discharge passengers on a schedule or on demand. Demand-responsive in the way an elevator is demand-responsive, it deposits the passenger on the street corner much as an elevator takes the patron to the floor of his choice. There are no emissions from the vehicle. PRT was at the top of the UMTA R&D agenda in 1969. In Morgantown, West Virginia, a potential demonstration site and user were at hand.

The Morgantown PRT project began in 1969 when the University of West Virginia asked for and received a research study grant from UMTA to see what could be done about its transportation problem. With three campuses approximately 1.5 miles apart, the university was forced to operate a bus system, supported by student fees, to shuttle students and faculty between campuses. Given the hilly, traffic-clogged, two-lane streets of Morgantown, travel was egregiously slow and expansion impractical. About 1100 students and faculty transferred from one campus to another for classes by means of 17 buses. They had to allow 70 minutes between classes to make this transfer. To improve the overall efficiency of its staff and facilities, the university wanted to reduce this transfer time significantly.

Relying on its own faculty and a transportation consultant, the university came up with specifications for a 3.2-mile, 6-station, computer-controlled PRT to move students and faculty between campuses. As well as solving its immediate problem, in the long run it would save money, since the PRT would be automated and thus bus drivers and other personnel necessary to operate a bus system would not be required. According to the consultant's estimates, the cost would be $13.4 million. What would solve West Virginia's problem would also solve a problem for UMTA. It would provide UMTA an opportunity to demonstrate a PRT in an exceedingly receptive setting. Secretary of Transportation John Volpe was personally quite excited by PRT and was pressing UMTA to start building hardware. Not only would a Morgantown demonstration help get PRT moving, it would also show Representative Harley Staggers, chairman of the House Commerce Committee and a man with strong influence on the DOT budget, that Volpe was doing something for him. Morgantown was in Staggers' district,[26] and the Commerce Committee was part of DOT's congressional subsystem.

In 1970, UMTA took control of the project, called it a demonstration program, and began funding the full costs. The Jet Propulsion Laboratory of Cal Tech was the initial prime contractor, with Boeing serving as subcontractor. "We're moving from study to action, from thinking to doing," declared Carlos C. Villarreal, UMTA administrator.[27]

Costs quickly began to go up, but the overruns tended to be attributed to earlier poor estimates by the university and its consultant. After SST was killed by Congress in early 1971, "senior Administration officials" were reported as having ordered DOT/UMTA to place Boeing in charge of the project. This was the first sign that new values attuned to partisan politics were beginning to invade those governing the developer-user system of UMTA/West Virginia University.

PRT now began proceeding on a crash basis. As a former UMTA official was quoted by the *New York Times:* "Volpe pushed everybody to have it running by the election."[28] PRT was paced in accordance with Nixon's electoral needs. The

---

26. Robert Lindsey, "U.S. May Raze Its $57-Million Showcase 'People-Mover'," *New York Times*, April 13, 1974, p. 1. Information on the Morgantown demonstration is based, in part, on an unpublished study in 1974 by Paul Flynn, a political science doctoral candidate in the Maxwell School of Syracuse University, as well as on interviews by the author.
27. *Ibid.*
28. *Ibid.*

goal was to have enough of PRT finished by November 1972 to hold a demonstration. Nixon could attend the dedication ceremonies, thus evidencing Presidential concern for urban transportation and the problems of the cities.

Millions were added to the cost as a consequence of the accelerated schedule. For example, the guideway was built before the weight of the passenger cars was known, and it was made far stronger than necessary. The cost was roughly $1100 a foot as against $150 a foot for a similar people-mover at the new Dallas-Fort Worth Airport. In addition, the complex computer-controlled system was reportedly rushed into hardware before it was tested. Meanwhile, as costs were added in some areas, project managers cut back in others—including performance. Siding planned for emergency use and provisions for pushing disabled cars were dropped. This meant that failure in one car would shut down the whole system.[29] Complicating and exacerbating all of these factors was another difficulty: much of the building of PRT had to take place in a busy downtown environment.

The effort was a political, if not a technological, success. In late October 1972, three weeks before the election, Tricia Nixon Cox, the President's daughter, joined Volpe in Morgantown to dedicate the system and set the first cars moving. National television reported the event on the evening news.

Immediately after the election, the top political executives of DOT and UMTA, like those of HUD, were replaced, and the new managers imposed a one-year moratorium on the PRT project. With the election behind, costs could now take precedence over speed, where the Morgantown demonstration was concerned. The costs now were considerable: over $115 million, if PRT were completed as originally planned by UMTA and West Virginia University. UMTA was anx-

---

29. *Ibid.* It should be noted that many of these unattractive revelations about the political impacts on PRT were made by Dr. Robert A. Hemmes, formerly UMTA's top transit research administrator. Hemmes was dismissed as a by-product of the Morgantown fiasco and obviously felt that he was taking the blame for decisions made "over his head" by the political estate.

ious to leave the problems of West Virginia behind and start afresh on a larger PRT demonstration in Denver. For its purposes, the Morgantown PRT was "complete." It had served as a national demonstration project. The technology "worked." On the other hand, the University of West Virginia complained that its transportation problem was still there and would not be solved by a system that was only half the scale of the original design.[30]

What had started out as an ideal partnership between UMTA, in its role as a technoscience agency, and West Virginia University, in its role as user in a national demonstration project, had so deteriorated by 1974 that the government and the university both were openly discussing razing a possible $57-million white elephant. This was not expected to happen—not with Staggers as a powerful broker between the agency and the user. It was assumed that a settlement would eventually be reached that would cost more than UMTA would like and provide West Virginia University less than it had originally expected to get.

Dial-A-Ride showed how politics at the bottom (state bureaucracy and unions) can delay a socio-technology program. PRT showed how politics at the top, in this case stemming from Presidential re-election considerations, can speed up a program. Sometimes Presidential interests can ease the way for R&D, but this was not the case for PRT. PRT became a pathological example of politicized R&D. It revealed the hurry-up-then-stop syndrome of a crash program followed by a one-year moratorium. The Presidential election was the variable. A technology that served the "user in the White House" in 1972 was of no interest to him in 1973.

CONCLUSION

The central problem that socio-technologies face is not technological, but political uncertainty. As has been shown in

30. Jack Magarrell, "University May Get a Blast Out of 'People-Mover' as U.S. Balks at Multi-Million Cost Overrun," The *Chronicle of Higher Education,* Vol. 8, May 13, 1974, p. 1.

the previous chapter, the same can often be said of high technology. But political uncertainty is all-pervasive in sociotechnology. It is the way of life of socio-technology, constant and unyielding. Cost overruns that would be ignored in high technology became scandals in socio-technology. What can be hidden under national security or esoteric technicalities is laid bare in the domestic/social realm. Although the public may stand in awe of space, weapons, and nuclear power, it is less impressed with prefabricated houses, buses, and fancy "people-movers."

The notion of two cultures—one in which the businesslike, rationalistic, technocratic mentality dominates administrative planning, and the other in which the purely political overwhelms all other considerations—is overdrawn, to be sure. Still, in many ways, the world of NASA and HUD do represent two cultures. How could Breakthrough's "scientific approach" be maintained under congressional budget-cutting, Presidential ambivalence, and the dismissal of HUD's top executives after only one four-year term? The role of top leadership in HUD was much more important for technology than that of similarly placed officials in high-technology agencies. HUD, like most domestic/social agencies, was only beginning to make technological innovation a part of organizational routines.[31] As suggested in Chapter 2, the "organizational capacity" to lead national technology programs of such agencies as HUD and UMTA leaves something to be desired. The lack of organizational capacity relates to bureaucratic power and, thus, to political support that is cognizant of the nuances and requirements of large-scale technology programs.

The best of technocratic dedication in building new technology avails little when the pace and direction of a program are determined (as was PRT) primarily in accord with short-range, partisan political timetables. R&D/demonstration pro-

31. See the report on HUD's efforts to mount an R&D program in James D. Carroll, "Science and the City: The Question of Authority," *Science,* Vol. 163, February 28, 1969.

grams take much time to reach fruition and to be applied in an operational framework. Indeed, it is harder to innovate in the "mature" (and often declining) industries with which domestic/social agencies are concerned than in the more open and vital territories of the high technologies. Socio-technocrats have far less time to develop and apply new technologies than their high-technology brethren. In reality, because the resistances are greater and the goals less clear-cut, they need more time to test and refine their tools. They need to be able to learn by experience, to experiment, even to fail. Otherwise, one demonstration will lead to another demonstration—but little else.

In high technology, the businesslike, rationalistic, and technocratic seem sometimes to dominate political decision-making. The politicians support or run interference for the technocrats. They take risks of the gravest sort, as in the arms race and civilian nuclear power. In high technology, the politicians may well do less than they should to check and balance technoscience power. In socio-technology, however, few politicians are willing to take the risks of supporting change. Although Senator Harrison Williams of New Jersey on the one hand, promoted urban mass transit R&D, on the other hand he made it possible to oppose the application of new technology through the leverage of the Department of Labor. As a consequence of this lack of support on the part of the politicians, socio-technology agencies are enfeebled at the outset in attempting to innovate. This is not to argue that technology is "the" answer to domestic ills. However, where it may help, it will not be applied unless strong, public organizations are created to steer the innovation through the multiple barriers of fragmented systems. To the extent that such agencies are weak and unable to protect their programs from the multifarious political pressures in Washington, the states, and the cities, they contribute to the problem of fragmentation. They are barriers to their own innovations.

5

Arresting Technology

IN THEORY, all technology development programs are born to die.[1] They are launched to produce particular new products or processes. When the intended result is achieved, demonstrated, and transferred, R&D policy concludes, and operational policy begins. In reality, many R&D programs never die—they just change their names. The most successful technology program from a technoscience agency's perspective would be one that was implemented in the manner and at the pace preferred by the agency and replaced by follow-on development programs aimed at producing later generations of the same technology. In this way, bureaucracy and its clients do not work themselves out of a function.

Some technology development programs die prematurely, others are killed, and still others are forced to remain incomplete, in the sense of never being fully deployed. While an agency itself may occasionally suppress a technology to suit its own purposes, there are many cases where the pressures for

1. Government programs may die. Technology *per se,* being a form of knowledge, is almost impossible to kill completely, although its development may surely be stifled or arrested. Government policy, by way of the Rural Electrification Administration, largely displaced windmill technology in the past several decades. Now, government policy is resurrecting this technology through R&D as a "wind energy system." See N. Wade, "Windmills: The Resurrection of an Ancient Energy Technology," *Science,* Vol. 184, June 7, 1974, pp. 1055–58.

constraining technology come from outside the organization charged with the development. Where and how much a technology program is stopped depends on the relative pressures for and against the technology. The process of halting technology is as important a facet of federal R&D policy as that of initiating and implementing technology. Although many programs are terminated (often prematurely), others may not be terminated soon enough. Then there are those that are neither ended nor completed; they live in the limbo of technological constraint. They are either held back by the low priority that they have in their own agency's budget or by the force of enemies outside.

The preceding two chapters have concentrated on the administrative politics of implementation, with emphasis on the relationships between developers and users. This chapter examines the dynamics of program survival, an interaction of technology's proponents and opponents. While the opposition has always been present in earlier chapters, here it is brought forward for special attention in order to facilitate a better understanding of the process by which federal technology programs are either contained or terminated.

CONTAINING TECHNOLOGY

Technologies languish when they are of low priority for their developers and potential users. They may be low priority because they have technical weaknesses, or perhaps they are politically controversial and not ripe for a strong push. They have some support, otherwise they would not exist at all. But they also have opposition, either inside or outside a technoscience agency.

INSIDE OPPOSITION

Inside opposition arises when an agency in establishing priorities is faced with various technical options. Behind technical options are institutional interests. To the extent that not all proposals can result in major technological programs, decisions that favor one program hurt another. This is particularly true where the options vying are different approaches to the same technological objective.

In Chapter 2, the launching of new technological programs was discussed. Attention was given to what happened to those technologies supported by their agencies. It was shown that they were pushed to even higher levels of decision, with national commitment the ultimate objective. What of the losers in technological choice? Once an agency makes a program decision in favor of one approach and against another, it may also support the losing technology, at least at a marginal level. There is organizational interest in keeping an alternative technology going, "just in case." Given the uncertainties of technological innovation there is always the desire to maximize organizational options. Moreover, agency leaders may wish to keep various segments of a large organization satisfied, if only to maximize cohesion behind lead programs. Usually, however, there are neither the funds nor the desire to support the alternative sufficiently to allow it to threaten the primary line of agency R&D.

For example, in 1961, AEC acceded to the desire of its Oak Ridge National Laboratory (ORNL) and assigned it the mission to develop a nuclear breeder technology called Molten Salt Reactor (MSR). This was but one of a number of routes to AEC's breeder goal. Another was the Liquid Metal Fast Breeder Reactor (LMFBR) which was then being developed at a sister AEC installation, Argonne National Laboratory. How early LMFBR was favored by AEC is unclear, but it is certain that once Milton Shaw became head of the AEC's Division of Reactor Development and Technology in 1964 the LMFBR's star ascended.[2] Shaw believed in making decisions and backing those decisions with resources and personal attention. Shaw learned his nuclear management from Ad-

2. Sheldon D. Strauss, "Our Fast Breeder Program . . . Where It Stands and Where It Is Going," *Nucleonics,* Vol. 24, December 1966, pp. 41–47. See also "Anti-Faret Decision Marks New Reactor Development Era," *Nucleonics,* Vol. 24, January 1966, p. 21.

miral Rickover and practiced it in AEC. By 1967 Shaw had the support of key leaders of AEC and the Joint Committee on Atomic Energy in advancing LMFBR as the principal technical solution to the country's long-term energy woes.[3]

MSR continued, although at a very low level compared with that of LMFBR. At the technical level of decision there was a question as to whether the agency and the country should place all of their bets on one particular approach to nuclear breeding. This was particularly the ORNL perspective—a point of view no doubt colored by its own institutional interests. On the other hand, it was also a view that had some backing higher in the organization, at least as long as there was plenty of money available.

When AEC won Presidential backing for LMFBR in 1971, MSR suffered. This was because the national decision to go with a breeder was not accompanied by a sufficiently large infusion of new funds to AEC to keep many approaches to that goal alive. MSR even created some potential public-relations problems for LMFBR. If AEC was so certain that LMFBR would work, why was it supporting alternatives? In 1973 AEC almost killed MSR completely. The decision was apparently made by the agency, which was forced to choose by OMB budget cutters. Aided by key members of the Tennessee legislative delegation, ORNL fought for a reprieve. The reprieve was granted, owing mainly to the Arab energy crisis and the beginnings of new money for AEC. Significantly, Shaw left AEC at this time. MSR survived.

Perhaps MSR may eventually triumph, a turnabout that would be a rare event in the bureaucratic world of science and technology. The normal fate of technological understudies is a lingering death. They may persist as alternatives to an agency's "main product line," but they do so only as long as the original choice is regarded as having technical uncertainties and the agency does not feel that the substitute is

---

3. Allen L. Hammond, "The Fast Breeder Reactor: Signs of a Critical Reaction," *Science*, Vol. 176, April 28, 1972, p. 391.

a threat to its first priority effort. Of course, outside pressure can keep some programs going at a low level of support, almost indefinitely.

INTERNAL/EXTERNAL OPPOSITION

Technologies can be contained at almost any point along the R&D/demonstration/deployment/use cycle. Under most circumstances, however, opposition pressures, external to the agency and its subsystem allies, come late. Undoubtedly, the great majority of containment decisions are made within the agency (frequently under OMB pressure) in the manner seen in MSR. Those technologies that are debated and contained *early* in R&D by outsiders are the exception, not the rule. Nevertheless, from the point of view of technological opponents, late containment is better than none at all. For example, nuclear critics have delayed to some extent the deployment of the light water reactor civilian nuclear technology. Their efforts have had the most telling effect at the point at which the industry itself sites a potential plant. From the perspective of the technoscience agency, this is late in the innovation process. However, as a byproduct, such actions have so raised the consciousness of environmentalists and other critics concerning nuclear energy as to have recently encouraged them to attack the breeder reactor while it is still in the development stage and in the direct province of the technoscience agency. Such early attacks remain the exception rather than the rule. Also it should be emphasized that the development of a breeder technology has been ongoing since World War II.

Thus, whether the subject is urban mass transit or nuclear weapons, opposition from outside of government generally comes late in the R&D process and often not until the technology is actually being tested, demonstrated, and deployed. In weapons technology, what successes arms controllers have had have usually been in containing the quantitative side of the military arms race rather than its qualitative aspects. One

of President Nixon's more positive contributions was decid-
ing to halt germ warfare research.[4] That qualitative decision
was notable for its rarity. The much more celebrated SALT
(Strategic Arms Limitation Talks) agreements of 1972, which
limited Anti-Ballistic Missile (ABM) deployment of both the
U.S. and the U.S.S.R., represent quantitative limitation. So
also does the 1974 agreement between America and Russia,
which put a ceiling on the number of nuclear weapons each
country could have in its arsenal at the end of ten years. Such
agreements on numbers did not check modernization (i.e.,
R&D). It is one of the deadly ironies of arms control that the
more that quantitative checks are placed on the contest between the two superpowers, the more the energies of the two
countries tend to be redirected toward R&D. While only one
ABM system has been deployed, respectively, in Russia and
America, each country continues research and development
to improve the technology of ABM.

This is not to denigrate arms control agreements at whatever stage they can be achieved. It is merely to suggest that the
outside politics of military technology containment usually
occurs at the deployment phase, while DOD and government
generally are the arena for weapons debate during R&D. As
has been suggested, one of the most important decisions in

4. There was a termination decision, but in the classified world of military
technology, there is always the possibility that such work is yet ongoing, in
secret. The halt of knowledge *per se* is exceedingly difficult. Recent breakthroughs in basic research in genetics have raised the potential for technologies
in germ warfare that millions spent for years in the *direct* pursuit of this goal
could not accomplish. This has occurred much to the dismay of leading researchers in the field. In 1974, a group of molecular biologists decided to take
matters into their own hands without waiting for government policy to crystal-
lize. They realized that they were on the brink of creating new forms of bac-
teria through genetic modifications that might be dangerous to humans since
there might be no known defense. An international moratorium was requested,
and the National Academy of Sciences called for a temporary ban on certain
kinds of experiments in genetics that might lead to the creation, inadvertently,
of a new germ warfare technology. See N. Wade, "Genetic Manipulation: Temporary Embargo Proposed on Research," *Science*, Vol. 185, No. 4148, July 26,
1974, pp. 332–34.

federal science and technology policy relates to the "readiness" of a technology to go from development to operations. The SALT decision to contain ABM's deployment was merely the culmination of a series of decisions, dating back more than a decade, that had as their purpose or effect the containment of ABM. Many of these decisions were made or largely influenced by the organization responsible for developing and deploying the system—the Department of Defense.

Within DOD, the key unit promoting ABM was the Army. In 1959 Secretary of Defense McElroy had divided the space and missiles roles among the three services and had assigned ABM to the Army. This was the only large, sophisticated missile program that the Army had.[5] Within the DOD system it was akin to the Oak Ridge Molten Salt Reactor program in AEC. It provided "pride of place" within the parent agency. It also gave tangible rewards for the scientific, technological, military, professional, and other "estates" directly involved in the huge program over the years.

Army was part of a larger organization—the Defense Department. As AEC had its priorities in reactor development, so DOD had its priorities in weapons. Secretary McNamara placed defensive weapons far down the list. Indeed, McNamara was firmly convinced that, whatever the technical questions involved, he should contain the ABM program lest a new defensive missiles arms race be unleashed to join the already massive offensive missiles race. As long as there were strong reservations among DOD technical people as to the efficacy of the system against Russia and as long as McNamara was extremely influential with the President, he was able to stop Army deployment efforts at the departmental level. The Army felt that ABM was "ready enough" for deployment and noted Soviet efforts to deploy an ABM around Moscow. Year after year, up to 1966, McNamara was strong enough to con-

5. Herbert York, *Race to Oblivion* (New York: Simon and Schuster, 1970), p. 214.

tain ABM decision-making within DOD and to keep the technology in a state of continuous R&D.[6]

The turning point came in 1966. Pressures to begin deployment were coming from a variety of directions. DOD's own top-level technologists were going along with a new rationalization being put forward by the Army: protection against a more limited Chinese offensive threat. At the same time, many legislators on the military committees in Congress were growing restive, in view of the deployment of an ABM system around Moscow. In this year, Congress approved $167.9 million for ABM procurement. The Secretary of Defense had not requested these funds and did not obligate them.[7] However, the Army and Joint Chiefs of Staff felt that the time was right to take their case beyond the Pentagon to the President. Their access to the White House had significantly improved, given President Johnson's growing concern with the Vietnam conflict.

At McNamara's urging, Johnson delayed decision, pending a Summit Conference with the Soviet Premier at Glassboro, New Jersey, in June 1967. There was no agreement on ABM at that conference, however. Johnson felt some need to make a move on ABM. Aside from the Russians, he had domestic political worries. He feared that the Republicans would use the "ABM gap" against him in the way he and John F. Kennedy had used the "missile gap" against them in the 1960 elections.[8] What he did was to make a "minimal" decision—one that had the effect of containing the ABM just a bit longer.[9]

6. The bureaucratic history of ABM is covered by Edward Randolph Jayne, II, "The ABM Debate: Strategic Defense in National Security," (Cambridge: MIT Center for International Studies, 1969). In addition, see "Chronology of the U.S. ABM Deployment Decisions, 1955–1969," in Abram Chayes and Jerome B. Wiesner, eds., *ABM: An Evaluation of the Decision to Deploy an Anti-Ballistic Missile System* (New York: Signet Books, 1969), pp. 227–35.

7. Chayes and Wiesner, *op. cit.*, p. 229.

8. See Morton Halperin, "The Decision To Deploy the ABM," in R. Head and E. Rokke, eds., *American Defense Policy* (Baltimore: Johns Hopkins University Press, 1973), pp. 466–85.

9. This decision should be compared with President Truman's decision on the H-bomb. See Warner R. Schilling, "The H-Bomb Decision: How To De-

His decision was to deploy a "thin" ABM system around selected U.S. cities. This was said to be an anti-China rather than an anti-Soviet system. It was a system that was less expensive and presumably less provocative to the Russians. It was not what the Army wanted, but it would do for the time being. ABM was now in the President's budget for deployment. Following congressional debate in 1968, approximately $1 billion was appropriated to begin the process.

Political controversy and the transition of national administrations in 1969 served to delay deployment, however. The controversy arose at the grass-roots level as well as in Washington. Many leading scientists, as individuals and through organized interest groups such as the Federation of American Scientists, were in the forefront of the opposition. The location of ABM sites around cities allowed opponents to mobilize protest groups from local campuses against ABM, as a symbol of misplaced national priorities, Vietnam, and a host of other military-related and technological concerns. This opposition mushroomed during the first half of 1969.[10] The Nixon administration's reorientation of ABM from city defense to missile defense may have defused some criticism, but it may also have ignited some additional opposition from those who were outraged at the notion of making ABM a "bargaining chip" in the SALT talks. In the summer of 1969, fifty Senators voted against ABM deployment, an exceptionally rare show of opposition to a major weapons program. The politics of ABM, once contained within DOD, had thus advanced to macropolitical levels.

How much the domestic-political debate influenced the U.S. position at SALT (if at all) is impossible to say. It is clear that SALT, in effect, froze ABM deployment where it stood. It limited deployment to two sites, one of which could be

---

cide Without Actually Choosing," in William R. Nelson, ed., *The Politics of Science* (New York: Oxford University Press, 1968), pp. 308–28.

10. Anne Hessing Cahn, "American Scientists and the ABM: A Case Study in Controversy," in Albert H. Teich, ed., *Scientists and Public Affairs* (Cambridge: MIT Press, 1974), pp. 41–120.

around the nation's capital. The U.S.S.R. system was deployed around Moscow. The U.S. ABM at North Dakota was virtually complete at the time of the SALT agreement in 1972, with another in Montana just beginning. The U.S. finished the North Dakota site, abandoned the one in Montana, and chose not to build a site around Washington. Later negotiations (SALT II) cut the number of sites permitted to one —in effect, the one each side already had. Had ABM deployment not been contained throughout the 1960's, first within DOD, then by the Presidential/congressional/domestic political process, there assuredly would have been more ABMs to contain at SALT, and the agreements might have been more difficult to reach.

It is significant also that, while debate over ABM reached macropolitical levels in the late 1960's, debate on the Multiple Independently Targetable Reentry Vehicle (MIRV) did not. A system which enabled one missile simultaneously to strike more than one target, MIRV was a major advance in weapons technology. It moved swiftly from development to operations with the locus of decision at the subsystem political level. As Luther J. Carter has pointed out:

. . . the chances of stopping MIRV began to fade in August 1968 when the United States began MIRV tests. Once the United States had bitten this particular apple of knowledge, the Soviet Union would insist on tasting it, too. Nevertheless, the decision to test MIRV was not even treated as a matter of Presidential importance—it went no higher than the office of the Secretary of Defense, then occupied by Clark Clifford.[11]

The Arms Control and Disarmament Agency (ACDA) tried to make MIRV an issue, but did not succeed. The national political process apparently had room for only one arms debate at a time. Ironically, the effort to contain ABM may have made it easier for MIRV to be deployed merely by focusing

11. "Strategic Arms Limitation (I): The Decades of Frustration," *Science,* Vol. 187, No. 4174, January 31, 1975, p. 331.

the spotlight of political debate elsewhere. Also, in the 1960's, McNamara's argument that the best defense was a strong offense, which he used against ABM, was used in turn against him within DOD by those who promoted MIRV and even more sophisticated and powerful offensive might.

TERMINATING TECHNOLOGY

Who terminates technology programs? How? When? Termination is the most extreme form of containment. A cancellation decision does not just stop a program; it ends it. Moreover, it drastically disrupts careers of those associated with it, including government administrators, private contractors, and scientists and engineers on the bench. The termination of large-scale technologies hurts regional economies. What causes pain locally triggers congressional rescue activity. The constituency of a large-scale technology program is never more in evidence than at the time of termination.

It is not just the effects of a termination decision on those whose jobs are directly and indirectly affected that make such decisions so significant. The real importance lies in the impact of the decision on the particular technoscience agency and, thus, the country. Ending a program closes off problem-solving options for government. Teams of federal and contractor executives and R&D performers break up and look for other work. Equipment is dismantled or redirected elsewhere. Ideas may be forgotten, and knowledge may go unapplied. Opportunities associated with the technology's promise are abandoned. A program termination decision cannot be taken lightly, and usually is not, by those in power to make such decisions.

Yet, terminations must be made. It is as important to kill programs that are of decreasing viability as it is to allow new programs to be born. The money that waning large-scale programs are using could better go to other live efforts or even to new programs struggling to be born. Keeping such old programs alive closes off new options. The uncertainties of R&D

require "learning," and it may take years before enough is
known about a new technology to realize that a further investment is no longer desirable. While the technology is advancing, perhaps another is also and is proving more "cost-
effective." Programs may be kept alive longer than warranted
because of sunk costs or sentiment or bureaucratic momentum. They may be killed, but only late in the R&D process.
Murray Weidenbaum has found that between 1957 and 1970
some 81 major weapons systems were cancelled, but not before $12 billion had been spent.[12]

To die, many programs do not require an overt, high-level
decision. They wither away, victims of decremental budgeting—for example, the Department of Transportation's high-
speed trains. These are usually the programs which a technoscience agency judges to be of low priority. While blame may
be placed on outside sources, such as the Office of Management and Budget, the agency itself cannot escape a role. If a
program is seen as low priority for the agency, it will be even
lower in the eyes of an organization whose mission includes
representing the President's interest in limiting bureaucratic
spending.

As the program's budget wanes, its constituency shrinks.
When the day of zero funding for a program arrives, there are
few to notice or to mourn. Consider the following terminations: the nuclear rocket, the nuclear airplane, and the supersonic transport.

THE NUCLEAR ROCKET

To discuss the demise of the Nuclear Engine for Rocket
Vehicle Application (NERVA) is to provide some understanding of the Byzantine politics of the Office of Management
and Budget (OMB) in relationship to technoscience agencies.
OMB helped send NERVA to its death in 1972. Yet it would
be over-simplifying to cast the long shadow of accusation—or

perhaps credit—on OMB. OMB works in ways that are very subtle and usually not visible to the outside world. It plays the role of institutional skeptic vis-à-vis bureaucracy. Year after year it subjects the various programmatic proposals of agencies to healthy criticism. It might *like* to kill programs, but it usually does not attempt to terminate them unless it feels that there is a good chance its decision will stand up before higher policy review. Whether that decision will stand up (i.e., be backed by the President) depends often upon OMB's reading of how hard the operating agency will fight for a program. That is key to understanding the politics of NERVA's cancellation. It involved an interaction among many supporters and foes of NERVA. In the final analysis what was crucial to the timing of the decision was the attitude of NASA toward the project. While, from the development side, it was a joint program (NASA and AEC), NASA constituted the user. Hence, the pacing factor in funding was NASA's *demand for* NERVA. How much did NASA *need* NERVA? The answer was "not enough" to sacrifice other, higher priority programs, *especially* the Space Shuttle, NASA's prize.

NERVA began officially in 1960, although it had grown out of other technology programs that had extended back to the mid-1950's. By the time of its demise it had consumed $1.5 billion. Before an operational system could have been built, another decade and another billion dollars might have been needed. NERVA would have peaked in funding at about the same time that Shuttle would be making its greatest demands on NASA and national resources. In 1971, OMB forced NASA to confront that fact, and when it did, NASA's support for NERVA weakened.

In marrying nuclear propulsion to rocketry, NERVA would have provided a source of power for very large space vehicles that would be capable of carrying men and equipment vast distances over long periods of time in outer space. When men first landed on the moon there were "heady predictions by space agency officials that the rocket would be needed as a supplier of lunar bases and the booster of manned flights to Mars."[13] However, in the early 1970's it became increasingly clear that there would be no lunar bases and no manned flights to Mars in NASA's foreseeable future. NASA would be the user of a system that would have no concrete mission when finally produced, at least no mission that presumably could not be accomplished just as well with chemical fuels.

The key year in the termination process was 1971. NASA had requested an overall $3.7 billion FY-1972 budget. OMB drew the line at $3.2 billion and requested NASA to revise its programs accordingly. When the agency did so, it downgraded NERVA. OMB took "NASA's apparent weakening of support for the program" as its "opening for a move to kill it once and for all."[14] OMB returned to NASA a budget that had close to zero funding for NERVA. NASA appealed to the President and thereby kept the program alive—but barely. It was cut by four-fifths. This meant that NASA could keep a skeleton crew working should it win a reprieve and an upgrading the following year. In the FY-1973 budget, however, NERVA was eliminated entirely. Friends of NERVA in Congress fought to restore the program, but there was little that they could do, with NASA no longer a strong ally on their side. NASA felt that it had no choice. As George Low, the agency's second in command, told Congress: "NERVA needs the shuttle, but the shuttle does not need NERVA."[15]

Who killed NERVA? The OMB? NASA? President Nixon? Congress, for not forcing NASA to change its priorities? The "people," for not clamoring for the lunar bases and missions to Mars that might have provided a rationale for NERVA? To ask who was responsible, ultimately, for the death of NERVA is to ask who was responsible for the changes in na-

13. Richard Lyons, "End of Rocket Project Produces Space Age Ghost Town," *New York Times,* March 26, 1972, p. 57.

14. Claude E. Barfield, "Space Report/Fund Cutback for Nuclear Rocket Engine Worries Space Program Backers in Congress," *National Journal,* May 29, 1971, p. 1160.

15. *Ibid.,* p. 1163.

tional priorities that left space in a fundamentally different bargaining position in the 1970's, vis-à-vis OMB, than it had been in the 1960's.

THE NUCLEAR AIRPLANE

The salient fact about the termination of the Aircraft Nuclear Propulsion (ANP)[16] program was that it happened twice. The first time, the decision did not stand and the project was revived. The initial decision to kill the nuclear plane came shortly after the Eisenhower administration came into power in 1953. The second occurred at the beginning of the Kennedy administration in 1961. At the time of the first decision the project was seven years old, and no nuclear-powered plane had been developed. At the time of the second decision the project was fifteen years old, and still no plane had been developed.

The Republicans had come to power in 1953 with the notion of balancing the budget, looking for "fat" in all the programs inherited from the Democrats. Defense was not excluded. Eisenhower's Secretary of Defense, Charles Wilson, targeted ANP for elimination. At that time, the program was in deep technological trouble because radiation hazards required thick shielding around the engine reactor that made the plane heavy and slow, thus not militarily useful. It would certainly not pass the military performance requirements of the Air Force, its destined user and AEC co-developer.

When Wilson made his decision, he ridiculed the nuclear plane, calling it a "shitepoke." Said the Defense Secretary, "That's a great big bird that flies over marshes, you know, that doesn't have much body or speed to it or anything, but it can fly." Immediately, the plane's friends—the Air Force, the AEC, the Joint Committee on Atomic Energy, and the industrial contractors—rallied to ANP's support. They argued that the effort should be continued. It should be reoriented,

16. For a more detailed account, see W. Henry Lambright, *Shooting Down the Nuclear Plane* (Indianapolis: Bobbs-Merrill, 1967).

if necessary, but to close off a technological policy option so soon was irresponsible. The manned bomber still looked like the best way to deliver atomic weapons. The long-range missile was, as yet, uncertain. Some leading scientists doubted the reliability and accuracy of the missile. The range of nuclear-powered flight would make ANP a competitor of the missile, a major factor in the minds of airplane proponents in the Air Force. Then, there was the specter of a Russian atomic plane, reported as being in the developmental stage by Defense Department intelligence operatives. Finally, from President Eisenhower's perspective, there was the administration's concern for the good will of the Joint Committee on Atomic Energy. If the Eisenhower administration were to go ahead with some of the initiatives planned in atomic energy, such as those seen in the 1954 legislation, it would need the support of JCAE. Killing one of the committee's pet projects did not appear to be the best way for a new administration to begin an important relationship. Thus, for a number of reasons, the nuclear plane did not die in 1953. Instead, it was "reoriented" from a development program to a research program. Whether the Wilson decision was actually reversed or just not enforced, the result was the same: continued life for ANP, albeit with a reorientation toward research.

The shift from development to research did not last. The pressures for "flying early" were too great. Because of the pull of the Air Force users, development specifications were defined by the Air Force, whether the technology was "ready" or not. As a consequence, ANP had a series of recurring "ups and downs" in funding and constant changes in requirements. The long-term effect was that the plane was kept alive by lowering military requirements to those that could feasibly be attained. The problem for ANP, however, was that, while this was occurring, the missile was coming into fruition. Moreover, conventionally fueled aircraft were also advancing dramatically. Still, the Eisenhower administration and the Joint Committee maintained the program. It was not until 1961, when a new administration came to power, that a fresh and severely critical look could be given ANP again.

Secretary of Defense McNamara decided ANP should go. However, there was still enough support in the Joint Committee and the Air Force to raise the decision to the Presidential level. President Kennedy listened to his science adviser and Defense Secretary, who stood against ANP; he heard the Joint Committee and the Joint Chiefs of Staff, who stood in favor; and, in the end, Kennedy decided against the program. This time, ANP's champions gave up. The environment of decision in 1961 was vastly different from that in 1953. The user, the Air Force, was not as anxious to have the plane in 1961 as it had been in 1953. The technical uncertainties that had loomed as barriers in 1953 were *still* largely to be solved. The more the plane's performance requirements had been compromised, the less useful the plane became as a military weapon and the less competitive it became, not only with missiles (now operational), but also with conventionally fueled long-range bombers.

The fact that a major fight was not waged to save the project was, indeed, significant. That the decision stood, relatively without contest, pointed up the degree to which the support for the project had withered away over the years, due to the many unfulfilled technical promises on the part of the plane's strongest allies. Not even renewed reports of a Russian atomic plane could rescue the American effort. Judging from events in succeeding years, the Russians, like the Americans, made a termination decision on the nuclear plane. Apparently, neither country wanted a "shitepoke" in its weapons arsenal.

THE SUPERSONIC TRANSPORT

Finally, there is the case of the Supersonic Transport (SST). As OMB and NASA were the principals in the demise of NERVA and Secretary McNamara and President Kennedy were in that of ANP, Congress was the principal in the decision to end the U.S. Supersonic Transport program. Here, a decision was made by Congress, not only against the wishes of the relevant technoscience agency, the Department of Transportation, but also against those of the President. Here, a Democratic Congress voted to end an activity initiated by one Democratic President, sustained by another, and supported by a Republican successor. The SST was another billion-dollar, decade-long development program. It was killed by Act of Congress in 1971. Why?

When President Kennedy authorized the program in the early 1960's, he did so because of international economic competition, prestige, and the general notion of American technological pre-eminence. These were important values in the post-Sputnik "New Frontier" period. That the intended users were private commercial airlines did not prevent the anointing of SST with national interest. While some of the problems connected with supersonic transport technology, such as the sonic boom, were noted early by technical specialists, these were not regarded as significant enough to negate a program decision at the Presidential level.

By the end of the 1960's, however, environmental values were surging to the top of the national agenda. A variety of environmental interest groups began to concentrate their attention on stopping the SST. They wanted a show of force in opposition to a form of technological "progress" that ignored deleterious human impacts. SST's managers had previously favored cost over environment in design decisions. Now they were faced with the consequences of those choices. Efforts to mitigate criticism (for example, promising not to fly over populated areas) did not assuage the antagonists. As time went on, the forces against the plane enlarged. Those in favor, such as the airline industry users, who would have been expected to have waged a strong campaign in behalf of the program, grew ambivalent. The companies were having difficulties making profits on another recent aircraft innovation —the Boeing 747. A number of businessmen, who were not overly worried about environmental considerations, questioned the plane on economic grounds.

In this new climate, President Nixon tried to establish a policy toward SST for his administration. He decided SST must continue to be implemented on schedule. Noting the joint French-British plane, as well as the Soviet SST, he felt that the United States could not be left behind in an area of technology in which it had traditionally been the leader.[17] Rather than ending the debate, the Nixon decision caused it to escalate and to transfer to the congressional arena. Increasingly, the issue was posed in symbolic political terms: technology vs. the environment. Senator Proxmire, once a lonely figure standing against the plane, suddenly found himself at the center of an ever growing array of allies. Much of his most telling ammunition against SST was supplied by scientists, some of whom suggested that the SST would impact adversely on the ozone of the planet and thus indirectly cause skin cancer. Another scientist, Richard Garwin, a member of the President's Science Advisory Committee, shattered the President's attempt to suggest unanimity for his decision within the executive branch. Garwin made known before Congress the technical and policy reservations which he had expressed in his role as a science adviser. Nixon's men were aghast. As one put it, "Who in Hell do those science bastards think they are?"[18]

In 1970 the plane barely survived congressional action. In 1971 Congress voted it down. Senator Proxmire explained the killing of the SST as a case where the people participated in a major technological decision. In his view, when the people learned how undesirable the program really was they decided that it was not worth the public investment. For Senators

17. Again, this points up the difficulty of really arresting a technology, rather than a given program. The U.S. SST may have died, but not the supersonic transports of other countries.

18. Daniel Greenberg, "David and Indifference," *Saturday Review*, September 30, 1972, p. 42.

Warren Magnuson and Henry Jackson of the state of Washington (home of the prime contractor, Boeing), the issue was thought to have been the misinformation provided "the people." For them also, the salient fact was public awareness and attention to the debate. As an aide to Magnuson declared after the termination vote:

Maggie and Scoop [Senator Jackson] called every Senator they thought they could influence this time. They called. They cajoled. They persuaded. They arm-twisted. They did everything they could, but you can't push something down the throats of the Senate. The SST became a big national issue, and it was just beyond the power of the senators to turn around.

Vote trading and arm-twisting are effective when the issue is not that big, when it isn't a glaring national issue. But it doesn't work when you've got the full focus of national attention on it. Then the pressure is on, as Senators will say, to "vote right."[19]

When a program goes macropolitical, as SST did, it broadens its constituency. The balance of power among friends and enemies in SST's subsystem had been supportive, but the new constituency was increasingly weighed against the program. As the opponents grew in strength, some friends backed off. Macropolitical issues generally wind up in Congress, the most "public" political body, for resolution. Change of national administrations is a key variable in terminations. In SST, however, the new President decided to continue, not cancel. What SST illustrates, therefore, is that Congress may also be a vehicle for change. This would appear to be particularly true if the locus of decision is shifted from the congressional subsystem level to that of Congress-as-a-whole.

To become subject to macropolitical debate, a specific technology must be brought into the spectrum of a broader national issue. Those who take an issue to Congress on appeal

19. *National Journal*, January 9, 1971, p. 27, as cited by Joel Primack and Frank Von Hippel, "Scientists, Politics, and SST: A Critical Review," *Bulletin of the Atomic Scientists*, April 1971, p. 27.

from the President must not only get their issue on the congressional agenda, but they must do so in a way that is politically salient, that will attract attention—and votes. The SST was made the nemesis of environment at a critical point in history when few legislators wanted to go on record, under the spotlight of national publicity, against the environment. In macropolitics, where Congress-as-a-whole is on display, the pressure is on, as the Magnuson aide said, to "vote right."

CONCLUSION

Why do some technology programs wither and die while others not only live but flourish? There are many reasons. One is that some technologies are bad ideas and it is remarkable that they get as far as they do before succumbing to the inevitable ax. Others, while potentially sound, are not ready for application. All of the promotion on the part of the Air Force for a nuclear plane could not change the limits on what could be accomplished, given the technological state-of-the-art. There might have been a nuclear plane, but it would not have been militarily competitive with conventionally fueled aircraft. Beyond the scientific and technological barriers, which did not deter decisions at the administrative level to proceed with the ANP, there are other factors that constrain or even terminate some programs. These stem from bureaucratic power, or lack thereof.

Technologies require organizational backing and resources if they are to be brought to fruition. Agencies can only promote so many programs at a given time. Hence, an important limiting factor, other than technology, is the priority of the technology for the sponsoring agency. Beyond that, there is the question of the priority of the agency in the nation-at-large. An agency may *wish* to promote a technology, but it may not have the power to do so, given opposition. Perhaps the agency views a technology as of low priority, but there might be outside pressures from subsystem Congressmen, potential users, or the OMB to give the program a higher priority. How successful the agency may be in resisting depends on its power relative to that of its antagonists.

There is a very subtle relationship between administrative and national levels of policy. For example, NASA might have wished to follow Apollo with a program aimed at landing a man on Mars, but such a notion was contained by the national priorities of the 1970's. It remained a NASA *plan*, but did not emerge as a *program*. There was no overt national policy decision to terminate the manned exploration of the moon with the end of Apollo. Yet, by the nation's failure to initiate a follow-on effort, the lunar program was cancelled, or at least delayed indefinitely. NASA's Space Shuttle had to be rationalized, not in terms of manned space exploration, but in those of utilization for earth applications. What occurred was a shift in national attitudes toward space and NASA. NASA had no choice but to adapt its programs and its priorities to its lessened role on the national scene. NASA pushed what it felt would be acceptable to higher-policy actors. National policy, thus, acted as a check on technological policy initiatives. It produced non-decisions by the technoscience agency.

Where opponents overtly contain or terminate administrative technology, they succeed because the agency's power base is weak. Thus, NASA was able to launch innumerable programs during the 1960's when it had a constituency that included the President, most of Congress, a host of industrial contractors, university grantees, the communications media, and its foreign competition, the Russians. When that constituency atrophied and NASA found itself with a smaller base from which to market its programs, NASA had to choose. It tended to concentrate its diminished power behind certain key projects, such as Space Shuttle, and to allow others, such as NERVA, to be terminated by the pressure of outsiders, in this case OMB.

Outside power is important in starting, maintaining, and stopping technology. There is almost always some opposition to major technology programs. Like bureaucratic power, however, outside influence tends to be mercurial. The environmentalists had the capacity to stop SST in 1971, but not the Alaska Pipeline a few years later. Environment had apparently given way to energy as a national priority. This suggests the rather uncertain role that "national policy" plays in technology. National politics (priorities) for science and technology do exist and change, but they tend to emerge almost accidentally through a complex interplay of events, public moods, the crisis of the moment, and bureaucratic initiatives.

Because power in administration is so evanescent, there is always the danger that one agency associated with a policy sector high on the national agenda at a particular time will have all of its programs accepted as "national policy," while another not so favored will be the victim of budgeteers looking for ways to save money wherever they can. The unevenness of power behind technology is striking. Just a wisp of opposition to a socio-technology program can cause it to be delayed, constrained, or even cancelled. Not even macropolitical debate could do more than contain the defensive missiles race.

6

Supporting and Using Science

THE EMPHASIS TO THIS POINT has been on technology. Science has been discussed, largely in connection with the development and application of technology. This also reflects the approach of government in contrast with the preferences of the scientific community. Spending priorities favor development first, applied research second, and basic research third. The emphasis in R&D for government is the same as that for industry. It is on applications. Thus, the question of basic research is always a special problem requiring particular attention to decisions and even to organizational structures. Last in government's R&D priorities, it is first in the priorities of the scientific community and in those of the performing institution most associated with basic research, the university.[1]

Virtually all the agencies with significant R&D expenditures allocate at least some funds to basic research. Yet, the justification must always be on faith, or hope. If the research is truly basic, it cannot be predicted to lead directly to a given end-product that the agency may want. The only product likely to emerge is a scientific paper published in a learned journal, often one incomprehensible to all but the author and

---

1. Harold Orlans finds that reversing R&D, making the dyad read "D&R," is more descriptive of the reality of federal science and technology priorities. "D&R Allocations in the United States," *Science Studies*, Vol. 3, April 1973, Brookings Reprint 273 (Washington, D.C.: The Brookings Institution, 1973).

his peers.[2] History suggests that this base of knowledge contributes ultimately to technological advance. The relationship may be far from direct, and the lag in years between research and eventual application may be measured in several decades. Hence, the recognized importance of basic research is equaled only by the problems that it causes agencies every year in "justifications." How to rationalize funds, whose values may not be shown to be tangible for a very long time (if ever), in a government that is politically attuned to very short-run, very practical considerations, is one serious issue in federal research policy. Another is how to manage such research, if it can be managed at all.

In fiscal year 1976, the President requested $2.3 billion for basic research. Was that enough? Which agencies should pay for which basic research fields? When should basic research give way to applied research? What is the role of basic research in agencies whose missions are other than the support of science *per se?* What is the role of the National Science Foundation (NSF), the one agency with a mission in basic research, in regard to applied research? What are the respective roles of such R&D performers as universities, non-profit research institutes, federal laboratories, and industry, in decisions regarding scientific research? Dael Wolfle calls universities the "home of science,"[3] but the presence on campus of the School of Agriculture testifies that the university has an applied, as well as a fundamental, research tradition.

ORIENTATIONS IN FEDERAL RESEARCH POLICY

The principal problems in federal research policy derive from the following factors. The central thrusts of government are toward applied research; those of scientists and universities are toward basic research. The federal government is accountability conscious; the scientists and their institutions

2. Daniel Greenberg, *The Politics of Pure Science* (New York: New American Library, 1967), p. 27.

3. Dael Wolfle, *The Home of Science: The Role of the University* (New York: McGraw-Hill, 1972).

prefer the maximum autonomy from controls of any kind. The government is problem-oriented; the scientific community is discipline-oriented. The pure scientist has an ideology that sustains him in the face of criticism from those who do not understand the importance of seeking truth for its own sake. The professional and institutional reward systems of scientists place emphasis on basic discovery. Applied research may benefit society, but it is not necessarily in the career-interest of the academic scientist.

Agencies are part of government, sustained by the public and presumably servants to its needs. Research agencies are not insulated from the pressures of the day for quick fixes to unyielding problems. They also deal closely with the research community, their clientele, and thus can understand that some problems do require a more general knowledge base before any solutions can emerge. Research agencies are, therefore, inevitably caught between the values of science and society.

Agencies tend to lean either in the direction of science-orientation or society-orientation in research policy. Over a long period of time these science-oriented and society-oriented styles are not necessarily in conflict, but in a shorter time span the administrative emphases are quite different. In extreme form, the two may be characterized as follows:

1. Science-oriented administration takes its cues from the values of the scientific community; society-oriented administration is attentive to interests of politicians and various research users.

2. Science-oriented administration *supports* research; society-oriented administration *purchases* research.

3. Science-oriented administration allows the scientists to take the initiative in pursuing their own curiosities; society-oriented administration gives the initiative to the agency, which is looking for solutions "targeted" to particular public problems.

4. Science-oriented administration permits scientists, often in determinative ways, to participate in choosing, through peer review, which proposals are funded; society-oriented administration chooses, through agency review, which proposals are funded.

5. Science-oriented administrators prefer to fund research through grants; society-oriented administration favors contracts.

6. Science-oriented administration considers *excellence*, in terms of scientific criteria in proposals, most important; society-oriented administration considers *relevance* to the agency's problems the key factor.

7. Science-oriented administrators like to deal with "colleagues" in universities, particularly the most prestigious universities; society-oriented administrators will deal with any institutional performer willing and able to meet their needs. To the extent universities are seen as less capable of performing in interdisciplinary, problem-focused modes and are less reliable than non-profit and profit-making firms in meeting deadlines, there may be a bias against universities in society-oriented administration.

8. Science-oriented administration takes a long-term view of its task. Thus, it will not only support research, but will build capability, both in individuals through fellowships and at universities through institutional grants; society-oriented administration works for more immediate solutions and seeks to use existing capability rather than to create new capability.

9. Science-oriented administration believes researchers can manage for themselves and minimizes formal reviews from Washington; society-oriented administration values accountability and responsiveness to agency views highly and, therefore, requires considerable "management" from Washington: site visits, frequent reports, "milestones," evidence of results getting to users, etc.

These two administrative patterns constitute abstractions

from reality. Few agencies reflect a totally science-oriented or a totally society-oriented style. However, as central tendencies in administrative behavior, they do serve as models which indicate ways various research agencies, or sub-units of agencies, shape their programs. What such patterns mean, in terms of the policy consequences of agency behavior, can be discerned through reference to concrete examples. We will discuss science-oriented and society-oriented research administrations as they are demonstrated by the actions, past and present, of three major actors on the federal research scene: the National Science Foundation (NSF), the National Institutes of Health (NIH), and the National Aeronautics and Space Administration (NASA).

SCIENCE-ORIENTED ADMINISTRATION

To whom or what are NSF and NIH responsible? Prior to 1968 the answer was: "To science." Since then, both agencies have become hybrids. In effect, they have two product lines, featuring both science-oriented and society-oriented administration. Given the utilitarian nature of American government and politics, it is remarkable that, as agencies, they could emphasize science-oriented administration for as long as they did. That they could was, in large part, because of the strategies of the agency leaders. Those strategies were quite different from one another, owing to the general subsystem/macropolitical settings of the agencies, as well as to the administrative styles of dominant personalities guiding them during this period. The two strategies were administrative self-restraint (NSF) and administrative activism (NIH). Both agencies were activistic about the goal of supporting science. Where they differed was in respect to means.

NSF: THE STRATEGY OF SELF-RESTRAINT, 1950–1968

Speaking of NSF during the apex of its science-oriented era, Sanford Weiner called it the "organizational manifestation of the 'scientific' norm: stressing the purity of basic research from application and the purity of NSF from politics."[4] NSF was not completely free from politics; it was part of the politics of science. It did refrain from using the normal bureaucratic strategies of empire building in order to increase support for its program.

Under its 1950 mandate, NSF had authority to promote basic research and education in the sciences, to support basic research, and to evaluate research programs undertaken by other federal agencies. It is clear that the authority to evaluate was not used. This lack of aggressiveness was symptomatic of the general approach of NSF to science administration during the 1950's and 1960's. For NSF, administration of science meant organizational self-restraint in playing a broader national policy role.

Appearing to go against general notions of bureaucratic imperialism,[5] such a strategy is understandable if one views it as a defensive strategy aimed at protecting the weak position of basic science in NSF. The strategy had its roots in NSF's scientific constituency—the scientific performers. This constituency did not wish to risk its privileged access with the agency. For NSF to think in more "national" terms might imply a greater applied, or society-oriented, administrative approach. This would mean a broader constituency of performers and also more attention to user considerations. Scientists were closely integrated into NSF's organizational decision-making structure through various part-time policy-making and advisory committees, ranging from the National Science Board, at the top policy level, to hundreds of peer-review experts associated with specific grant programs.[6]

4. Sanford L. Weiner, "Resource Allocation in Basic Research and Organizational Design," *Public Policy,* Vol. 20, Spring 1972, p. 242.

5. See Matthew Holden, " 'Imperialism' in Bureaucracy," *The American Political Science Review,* Vol. 60, December 1966, pp. 943–51.

6. David Allison captured the essence of NSF in 1966 when he stated: ". . . the Foundation is not Director Leland Haworth nor the 300 professional people with scientific backgrounds who make up his staff. Practically speaking, the Foundation is Haworth, his staff, *plus* the 24 members of the National Science Board, *plus* some 39 advisory panels, division committees, councils, ad-

The scientific community pressed the agency to be a *National Foundation for Science* rather than a *Science Foundation for the Nation.* The flight from national bureaucratic power complemented a science-oriented administrative strategy. The more NSF refrained from society-oriented applied research, the more firmly it became a captive of the scientific community. NSF's years as a paragon of science-oriented administration are significant in revealing administrative tactics of self-restraint, such as narrowing jurisdiction, limiting constituency, and establishing an appropriate administrative ideology.

Narrowing Jurisdiction. NSF was born into a policy space filled with other research organizations. Alan Waterman, the first NSF director, had come from the Navy's principal research bureau, the Office of Naval Research. This agency was already a major power in science-oriented administration, having preceded NSF in establishing close ties with the academic science community by several years. Waterman well knew that jurisdictional territory, once gained, would not easily be relinquished by a technoscience agency. To have claimed expertise across the gamut in science policy and administration would have required a confrontation with administrators of science programs in a host of other agencies, most of which were much larger than the newly formed NSF. NSF was thus in a defensive position. The National Institutes of Health were entrenched in life sciences. In addition to the

---

visory committees, and so on, which are made up of several hundred scientists and engineers who represent various technical fields and who come to the Foundation periodically to advise on new programs and to evaluate the proposals that have been submitted by *other* scientists and engineers." David Allison, "The National Science Foundation," *International Science and Technology*, No. 52, April 1966, pp. 76–78, 80, 82, 84, 86. Under the NSF Act of 1950, it was unclear as to where the NSF director looked for policy guidance. The National Science Board was a policy-making body apointed by the President, but this was a part-time organization. It did not appoint the director—the President specifically retained that power. President Truman had vetoed an earlier bill that would have made the director an appointee of the board. What was ambiguous in form was not in practice, for NSF directors acted as though they were responsible to science, and scientists dominated the board.

Navy, the Air Force and Atomic Energy Commission were also active in the physical sciences.

Where would NSF fit in? The logical answer was: "Where others are not." For NSF the essence of science administration ultimately meant filling gaps between other agencies. In so doing NSF was placed in the position of supporting research that was least relevant to any mission-oriented goal. This suited NSF. What was least relevant to the other agencies could be considered as being most pure, and NSF was in the business of pure research.

NSF avoided expansion of jurisdiction into applied areas, even when there was little competition from other agencies. In 1958 Congress directed NSF to mount a program in weather modification R&D. The agency was instructed to engage in applied as well as basic research. As a subsequent congressional study found, NSF did not change its operating procedures to meet the congressional demand. Instead, NSF changed the weather modification program to meet its SOP's. Weather modification was treated as a basic research activity within the broader field of atmospheric sciences. This was not what the politicians in Congress had wanted—but it was what NSF and its scientific-performer constituency wished to do. Congressionally provided jurisdiction was thus narrowed by administration. Legislative purpose was tailored to organizational/clientele routines.[7]

Limiting Constituency. NSF did not want to enlarge its jurisdiction, and thus its constituency. As a "national" independent agency, NSF had no specific operational function. It was charged with science support, in general. It was usually distinguished from the mission agencies (e.g., DOD, NASA, HEW). NSF, of course, did have a mission: science support. This mission was so broad, so diffuse, so "national" that it was hard to define, apart from a specific concern for the care and

7. For NSF and the politics of weather modification, see W. H. Lambright, "Government and Technological Innovation: Weather Modification as a Case in Point," *Public Administration Review,* Vol. 32, January/February 1972, pp. 6, 7.

feeding of science and the university. NSF had no obvious user constituency, save the President (for national science policy) and researchers who built on the work of other NSF-funded performers. By its decisions, by moving into applied areas, NSF might have built a broader, more applied constituency to go along with the performers. It might have used its direct access to the President as a means to gain his support and that of his broad national clientele. As for Congress, NSF saw only its appropriations committees. Under its founding legislation it was not obligated to go through an annual authorization process. It might have enlarged its legislative constituency by distributing grants with an eye to geographical spread and congressional support. It might have cloaked the basic research in applied-sounding names. NSF, however, refused to engage in such "politics."

Although the only politics for NSF was in that of the scientific community, it discovered that too close an association with even the best of scientists could lead to administrative disaster. This was seen in the Mohole fiasco. Mohole, the drilling of the deepest hole in history, had pure science as its goal. It was endorsed by some of the nation's most illustrious earth scientists. It was wrapped in the prestige of the National Academy of Sciences. How could NSF, so devoted to its scientific constituency, refuse a project so high on the agenda of science? It could not.

In the interest of science, NSF chose a course it had so definitely avoided in weather modification. It became embroiled in large-scale technology and all the complications surrounding such efforts. The goal to penetrate beneath the earth's crust to reach the mantle, which comprises about 85 percent of the planet's interior, was pure science. The means for getting there was pure technology. NSF, accustomed to the relatively passive administrative style of reviewing and funding small basic-science proposals, was not equipped in personnel or managerial experience to run big technology projects. The results were cost-overruns, slippages in schedule, and fights among scientists, engineers, and contractors for control and direction of the program. There was controversy, both in the executive branch and in Congress. Eventually, Congress cancelled the project.[8]

There was a difference in the way NSF perceived projects. This difference seemed to depend upon who proposed the project. In the weather modification case, an excluded constituency (the politicians) had pushed. In the Mohole project, pure scientists were the prime movers. NSF, having gone its accustomed way in the Mohole project, found itself a victim of its own bureaucratic preferences.

Establishing an Administrative Ideology. To buttress its administrative strategy, NSF evolved an appropriate ideology. In any agency the first leader can design the basic plan, cement the building blocks of organizational philosophy, and recruit personnel who will work well within the ideological structure he has conceived for the organization. This individual, more than any other (especially if he can hold office a number of years), can help infuse the specific values that make an organization into an institution.[9] Waterman presided over NSF for its first thirteen years. The Waterman style became the NSF style, and this style was what the scientific community, through its elite on the NSF board and advisory panels, wanted.

Waterman *believed* the scientific ideology: science should be pursued for its own sake, under the maximum freedom for

---

8. The Mohole story is recounted in Daniel S. Greenberg, *The Politics of Pure Science, op. cit.,* Chapter 9. See also the same author's "MOHOLE: The Project That Went Awry," in Sanford A. Lakoff, ed., *Knowledge and Power* (New York: The Free Press, 1966), pp. 87–111.

9. As Philip Selznick notes: ". . . in administrative agencies, technical programs and procedures are often elaborated into official 'philosophies.' These help to build a homogeneous staff and ensure institutional continuity. Sometimes they are created and manipulated self-consciously, but most administrative ideologies emerge in spontaneous and unplanned ways, as natural aids to organizational security. A well-formulated doctrine is remarkably handy for boosting internal morale, communicating the basis for decisions, and rebuffing outside claims and criticisms." Philip Selznick, *Leadership in Administration* (New York: Harper & Row, 1957), p. 14.

the investigator. He felt that the best research administration was that which managed science least. Waterman had little interest in making *national* science policy. "National policy for science is a matter primarily to be determined by the scientists themselves," he wrote.[10] Further, "In any recommendations . . . concerning a research effort of the country, any agency, public or private, should defer to the judgment of the active and capable research scientists in that field.[11] There would be no "selling" of science, under more society-oriented labels, for Waterman:

I believe we must . . . establish the inherent rightness of basic research in and of itself. Once that philosophy enjoys common acceptance, I believe we shall have no difficulty in persuading members of Congress . . . that basic research is important and necessary on its own right, and not only because it eventually pays off in very practical ways.[12]

The dominant consequence of the strategy and tactics of self-restraint was a measure of autonomy for NSF in supporting science in the way it thought best. The drawback of this approach lay in the amount of money it brought NSF and, thus, science. In fiscal year 1966, at the height of science-oriented administration in NSF, the agency was spending only $290 million for basic research. The federal total for basic research was $2.2 billion. In other words, other federal agencies accounted for almost 90 percent of the total federal

10. "National Science Foundation: A Ten-Year Résumé," *Science,* Vol. 131, May 6, 1960, p. 1342.

11. U.S. Congress, House Committee on Science and Astronautics, 89th Congress, 2nd Session, report prepared by the Science Policy Research Division, Legislative Reference Service, Library of Congress, *The National Science Foundation: A General Review of Its First Fifteen Years* (Washington, D.C.: US-GPO, 1966), pp. 24, 25. Hereinafter cited as U.S. Congress Report, *NSF: Its First Fifteen Years* (1966).

12. A. T. Waterman, "First-Year Plan of the National Science Foundation," *Proceedings of the Fifth Annual Congress on the Administration of Research* (Ann Arbor: University of Michigan, 1952), p. 68. Cited in Weiner, *loc. cit.,* p. 246.

basic research, justifying that support in terms of practical missions.[13] NSF may have been pure, but it was also poor.

NIH: THE STRATEGY OF ADMINISTRATIVE ACTIVISM, 1945–1968

Unlike NSF, NIH was located in a larger unit of government, the Public Health Service (PHS), an organization of the Department of Health, Education, and Welfare. According to the hierarchical relationships, it appeared that NIH would be oriented to the mission of PHS, rather than to that of basic scientists. Actually, for approximately two decades with but a few programmatic exceptions, NIH was to life scientists what NSF was to physical scientists: a public foundation utilized primarily for private purposes.

In 1965 a number of illustrious members of the scientific community studied the administration of NIH and declared in the "Wooldridge Report":

Its internal structure continues to suggest that it is almost exclusively concerned with waging a series of campaigns against specific disorders like cancer, heart disease, or mental illness. Its position within the government suggests that it is regarded as the research arm of the United States Public Health Service. . . . It is in fact much the largest and most significant single institution for the promotion of the life sciences in the world.[14]

The writers pointed out that the primary *de facto* mission of the agency was the stimulation and support of a very broad range of health-related or biomedical research, "hence, such labels as 'heart,' 'cancer,' 'neurological diseases and blindness,' and the like, in the title of the major organization units of NIH, suggest more of an orientation to specific diseases than actually exists." The report lauded the NIH manage-

13. U.S. Congress Report, *NSF: Its First Fifteen Years* (1966), p. 52.
14. *Biomedical Science and Its Administration,* the Wooldridge Report to the President (Washington, D.C.: USGPO, 1965), p. 210. Cited in Weiner, *loc. cit.,* p. 252.

ment for "making a scientifically inappropriate organizational structure an effective arrangement for performing its real mission."[15] Seldom has a scientific study group more revealingly explained the reason for NIH's long-standing financial success. It lay in its capacity to justify a politically weak mission (pure research) via one of great salience (better health). NIH is the major federal agency for support of the life sciences. If NIH support were to be taken away, much of the research base of university medical schools and life science departments would collapse.

Like NSF, NIH is more than an agency. The "Wooldridge Report" stated that during the 1950's and 1960's NIH had become the "most significant single institution for the promotion of life sciences in the world." Its budget had soared from $50 million in 1950, to $430 million in 1960, and to $1.4 billion in 1967. It was thus a wealthy, finely honed, administrative tool "infused with value."[16] It was infused with the values of the scientific community, whose professional values were shared by the NIH leadership. Knowing their goals, NIH officials planned accordingly over the years. It takes time, money, a degree of autonomy, and a loyal constituency to build an institution out of a government bureau, and NIH had all of these resources. It also had a strategy: a strategy of administrative activism. From 1945 to 1968 NIH revealed how societal interests could be manipulated to bolster a basic research mission. It showed how the following tactics could be applied: building a public consensus against an "enemy"; channeling a substantial public interest; packaging a product; and using subsystem constituents.

Fighting the Enemy.   NIH was able to utilize the consensus *against* dread disease as a means to obtain funds *for* basic

15. Cited by Stephen Strickland, "The Integration of Medical Research and Health Policies," paper presented at the American Association for the Advancement of Science Conference, December 28, 1970. See also Stephen Strickland, *Politics, Science, and Dread Disease* (Cambridge: Harvard University Press, 1972).
16. Philip Selznick, *Leadership in Administration, op. cit.,* p. 17.

research. Urgency and thus money are added if a mission is associated with a perceived threat. As national security provides incentives to defense research, the element of personal security makes health research more salient than other areas of public science.[17]

Channeling Interest. There was sufficient controversy about the applied side of the health mission (delivery) to make it feasible and easy to channel support toward research. During the period of NIH ascendance as a basic science agency, strong and effective resistance by the American Medical Association to any major federal measures on the delivery side of health care meant that health interests were directed toward areas of least dispute.[18]

Packaging a Product. In 1955, the NIH National Microbiological Institute was renamed the National Institute of Allergy and Infectious Diseases. The Institute had been handicapped in making its case to the appropriations committees because "no one ever died of microbiology."[19] Moreover, what the scientists who wrote the "Wooldridge Report" in 1965 regarded as "a scientifically inappropriate organizational structure" was actually the perfect package for an agency located in a department with an applied mission. Here was science-oriented administration in a society-focused setting. That NIH was putatively the research arm of PHS (which, in turn, was part of HEW) helped in appropriations. It added to the credibility of the mission orientation of NIH. As NIH gained in funds and constituency, PHS lost effective power over it. As the power of the science arm grew, that of the mission organization withered, in relative terms.

Using Subsystem Constituents. NIH had political support that included friendly, powerful appropriations subcommittee chairmen and, unlike NSF, a two-party, interest-group

17. Strickland, "The Integration of Medical Research and Health Policies," *loc. cit.*

18. *Ibid.*

19. Harold Seidman, *Politics, Position, and Power*, 2nd edition (New York: Oxford University Press, 1975), p. 35.

constituency. The two parties were performers and users of NIH research. There was longevity among the principal actors in this constituency. The various actors in leading roles were "career people," with all the expertise, skills, contacts, and equilibrium relations that the term implies. When the principals in the health research subsystem agreed, their choices were approved by the larger political system. From 1955 to 1968, James Shannon presided over the agency. These were the years of maximum growth and autonomy as a basic research institution. He had extraordinarily good relationships with Representative John Fogarty and Senator Lister Hill, his key appropriations subcommittee chairmen. These two legislators showered money on NIH, consistently giving more than any President requested. More often than not, Presidents—and thus the Bureau of the Budget—acquiesced to congressional wishes when it came to biomedical research funding. To do otherwise was to appear to be against health research.

Another key individual in the NIH subsystem was Mary Lasker, the philanthropist, whose husband died of cancer in 1952. Over the years, she and her Foundation have been dominant forces on the user side of the constituency of NIH. As Weiner has described the tactics of the Lasker Foundation, they constitute:

. . . a well-organized, multifaceted effort. The Lasker Foundation puts out studies on the costs of major diseases and the benefits of medical research. It makes awards to Congressmen and medical writers for "advancing interest in health." A professional lobbyist (Tom Gorman) works in Washington and helps arrange for selected well-known doctors to testify before the Appropriations Committees on the need for increased research funds. Gorman's relations with Congressmen are aided by the fact that "Mrs. Lasker is known to be one of the nation's most generous campaign contributors." Gorman is also expert at the "White Paper device." Nearly all the White House and Congressional panels on health in the last twenty years have included Mrs. Lasker or her expert allies. Their reports, sometimes written by Gorman, invariably supported more research.[20]

The user-oriented groups were helpful allies of the agency only so long as their applied interests were kept in check. While they were given access, including representation on various NIH committees, the agency leadership retained dominant influence over policy direction.

The other side of the interest-group constituency, if not so openly active, was potentially powerful. The performer constituency of NIH included the nation's medical schools and their high-status doctor researchers. Even the in-house researchers of NIH were formidable, as they included some Nobel prize winners. It was to the performer interests that NIH, as a self-conceived, basic research agency, sought to be most responsive. Shannon has candidly stated that his ambition at the time was to establish a sound, high-quality, scientific base in this country, and that the needs of society *per se* did not figure directly into the equation.[21]

The NSF and NIH cases of science-oriented administration represent contrasting situations. In one, it meant independence from a functional, mission-created responsibility, but it also meant a relatively impoverished existence. In the other, the applied setting permitted considerable funds, but at the expense of what might be called "truth in packaging."

After 1968, three of the major figures in the NIH subsystem were gone: Shannon, Hill, and Fogarty. Mary Lasker remained and was instrumental in moving the organization toward a more society-oriented mode. There was no doubt that NIH, like NSF, accomplished a great deal for science. The problem with science-oriented administration is that it takes time to realize a return on the public's investment. Near the end of the 1960's, the "Laskerites" and key elements in the

20. Weiner, *loc. cit.,* p. 250.
21. Barbara Culliton, "NIH: Who Is Running the Show—Scientists or Politicians?" *Science,* Vol. 183, March 1, 1974, p. 830.

political estate grew impatient. In the 1970's this impatience increased.

SOCIETY-ORIENTED ADMINISTRATION

The society-oriented style of research administration clearly gained headway in NSF, NIH, and all other federal agencies. In 1968, new NSF legislation emphasized congressional intent that the agency become more society-oriented. To strengthen the impact of the user-interest on the agency, the legislation required NSF to go through annual authorization hearings, as well as appropriations hearings. In effect, the legislation imposed a two-party, interest-group constituency, with Congress indicating it would represent user concerns in the new NSF subsystem. In NSF, the organizational embodiment of the applied emphasis was the Research Applied to National Needs (RANN) program. In NIH the "war on cancer," established by 1971 legislation, was the most predominant symbol of change. Although both agencies strove to remain primarily science-oriented in style, the new suborganizations were the areas within which substantial growth was occurring, not only in budget but, more importantly, in ideological influence on the agency-as-a-whole.

A new cadre of personnel came aboard NSF and NIH. These were men and women from NASA, think-tanks, and industry, with systems-analysis techniques and cost-effectiveness jargon. NSF and NIH were not getting into "development" *per se,* but they were becoming more applied in orientation. "Targeted research" became a fashionable concept in federal science administration.

THE NIH SPECIAL VIRUS CANCER PROGRAM

What little evidence existed concerning the implications of the new effort to "manage" science was not altogether reassuring. There had been a program of targeted research in NIH during the 1960's. This was one of the exceptions to the general, science-oriented style of the agency. It had been established as a result of particular legislation. Beginning in 1964, the Special Virus Cancer Program (SVCP) of the National Cancer Institute of NIH poured millions into targeted basic research in an effort to discover the role of viruses in cancer and the ways to mitigate their adverse effects. As to the success of the program the program managers in NIH and many of the nation's leading cancer researchers have differing opinions. Reports appearing in *Science* magazine,[22] based in part on the study of the virus cancer program by a select committee of the National Cancer Advisory Board,[23] indicated that in managing the program the National Cancer Institute administrators had narrowed the scope of the effort. This was probably desirable if the means to the end were well understood. However, in the view of many cancer researchers, including those on the special committee investigating the program, the time was *not* ripe for the program goals to be attained.

The 1974 report by the special committee noted that the program had been in operation ten years and had spent a quarter of a billion dollars. It commented that proponents of the program incorrectly assumed that sufficient knowledge existed to mount a narrowly targeted program when, in fact, there was not sufficient knowledge to do so. Moreover, the managers of the program were also researchers, who controlled their own in-house facilities and, thus, were actively interested in testing pet theories of their own. Scientists on the outside, who did not share those theories or refused to adapt their style to the administrative demands of Washington, tended not to be funded.[24] *Science* quoted the report, which at that time had not been publicly released, as saying:

22. Nicholas Wade, "Special Virus Cancer Program: Travails of a Biological Moonshot," *Science,* Vol. 174, December 24, 1971; Barbara J. Culliton, "Cancer: Select Committee Calls Virus Program a Closed Shop," *Science,* Vol. 182, December 14, 1973.

23. Report of the *ad hoc* Committee To Review the Virus Cancer Program to the National Cancer Advisory Board (Bethesda, Md.: National Cancer Institute, June 1974). Referred to as the "Zinder Report."

24. Barbara J. Culliton, "Cancer: Select Committee Calls Virus Program a Closed Shop," *loc. cit.*

It was only natural that when the SVCP was formed a small group of investigators was involved—an "in-group." It now represents a somewhat larger "in-group" of investigators. Administratively, its procedures lack vigor, are apparently attuned to the benefits of staff personnel, and are full of conflicts of interest. Because the direct targets have become fuzzy since 1964, although available funds for the program continued to grow, the program seems to have become an end in itself, its existence justifying further existence.[25]

Was the SVCP really a "closed shop" or was the view that it was closed merely the manifestation of a resentment on the part of the excluded elements of the scientific community to a mode of administration they did not like?[26] The answer was important because, despite criticism and efforts by NIH top officials to reform the program, the programmatic style was similar to that which was being used in the much larger war-on-cancer effort that began with the cancer legislation of 1971. Society might *want* a cure for cancer, but, if the means were not known, would an Apollo-style approach yield results or would it merely produce a great deal of work for scientists willing to conform to roles that an agency had preselected for them?

The aim of applied, or targeted, research administration is to require scientists to work more directly and immediately on society's goals rather than on their own disciplinary objectives. What happens, however, when the goals of the federal *research managers* tend to come between those of society and those of scientists? The scientific community at times may well lose sight of the broader purposes for which its work is being funded. The same problem may also occur when research "managers," who should be acting on behalf of society,

25. *Ibid.,* p. 1111.
26. Dwight Waldo has noted to the author that, even in science-oriented administration, there is always an "in-group"—at least to those in other institutions and/or with different paradigms.

design programs that suit their own research interests and the objectives of those scientists in agreement with them. Closure is potentially as much a pathology of society-oriented administration as it is when an agency is overly responsive to the scientific community. Society's needs may be ignored as easily by research plans initiated by administrators as by scientists. This may be particularly the case when the administrators regard themselves as scientists who know "the one best way" to a given end.

NASA AND THE USE OF UNIVERSITIES

Both science-oriented and society-oriented research administration focus on *scientists*. The principal link between governmental and scientific interests is the project grant or contract. In form, federal project funds go to an institution; in reality, the money is controlled by specific researchers. This is especially the case in the university, where the separation between faculty and administrators is rather extreme. In fact, the actual research administration of a university is often reduced to performing a clerkship role for the faculty members. The award of funds to the university, as such, is usually but a nominal arrangement. What the federal agency wants is either to support an outstanding scientist or to purchase work from him through a contract.

In the 1960's, however, a form of research administration evolved that was "university-oriented" and was distinctly different from either mode thus far discussed. This was the "institutional grant," which was employed by various agencies as a supplement to their project grants and contracts. The aim was to aid universities in maintaining coherent research programs in the face of fragmenting tendencies of the project system. Institutional awards provided university administrators with discretion in allocating funds over very broad areas of research. An important purpose was to strengthen universities, as such, and administrators of universities, in particular. Be-

fore the burgeoning of the Office of Education's funding for
higher education in the latter 1960's, the institutional grant
was a means to aid higher education in the name of science.
For the most part institutional grants were ideologically a
form of science-oriented administration. The aim of the
grants was to support the institutions of science. Under
NASA, however, the institutional grant aimed not only at
support but also at institutional change and the application of
university resources to societal problems. The NASA program thus presented a glimpse at an attempt at society-
oriented administration on the scale of the university-as-a-
whole. In the 1970's one reason many research administrators
deliberately veered away from universities as institutional
performers was their conclusion that the NASA experience
had been a failure.[27]

With the Sustaining University Program (SUP), which ran
from 1962 to 1970, NASA provided funds for fellowships and
research grants that permitted wide discretion on the part of
university administration as to how that money was used. In
addition, it supplied new buildings, with no requirements for
matching funds. These buildings, or "facility grants," did not
go to the poorer institutions of American higher education;
they went to the nation's leading research universities. And,
instead of requiring matching funds, NASA required something else.

The university presidents, who received a "space" building, co-signed an agreement—a Memorandum of Understanding—with NASA's administrator, James Webb, in which they
agreed that they would attempt to bring their institution into
direct and effective service of society in practical and visible
ways. They also agreed to encourage their university researchers to assist in the utilization of research by the industries in
their regions, to promote new industry and economic growth,

27. For a more detailed analysis of the NASA university effort, see W. Henry
Lambright and Laurin L. Henry, "Using Universities: The NASA Experience," *Public Policy*, Vol. 20, Winter 1972. This section is based largely on
that article.

and to apply knowledge derived from NASA experience to governmental and societal problems, including that of the growing urban crisis. In promoting intellectual and organizational unity in the universities and in strengthening their leaders, Webb, who had conceived the effort, hoped for the emergence of interdisciplinary, problem-oriented, institutional capability and a feeling of responsibility for meeting new societal challenges. In other words, Webb saw SUP as aimed not only at building a *science* base, but also at using a *university* base for social betterment. This was society-oriented research administration on a large scale. Apparently he believed that if NASA had the capability to innovate in technology, it had the capability to bring about innovation in perhaps the slowest to change of all R&D performer institutions.

Webb did not cite specific models or precedents, but it was obvious that he had been impressed by such developments as Route 128 in the Boston area, the North Carolina Research Triangle, and the Southern California aerospace complex. Implicit in SUP's service notions were such precedents as the land-grant college, the "Wisconsin idea," and the University of North Carolina's long-standing concern with regionalism. There could also have been foreshadows of the "relevant" university that began to be demanded by reformers in the late 1960's.[28]

Webb thought an enhanced concern for its social responsibility would be good for the university and society, as well as for NASA. If the universities could become more effective in economic development and otherwise meeting the needs of their respective regions, then the leaders who controlled the resources of those areas would come forth with generous support to the universities. Fostered by NASA, such developments would work more quickly to diffuse the fruits of space research in economically useful ways, would better show the value of the nation's investment in space, and thus would assure NASA of increased political support. Where Webb was

28. *Ibid.,* p. 70.

concerned, it was impossible to separate the ideals of a social engineer from the realism of a practical bureaucratic politician.[29]

Webb conceived SUP as society-oriented administration at its best. How his subordinates saw the program is difficult to say. It appeared to be run more as a traditional program of institutional aid to the university than an effort to "redeploy" the university from outside. Certainly the university saw SUP as just another institutional grant program. By every standard by which "traditional" institutional grant programs were then measured, NASA was successful. Thousands of Ph.D.'s were trained (perhaps more than were needed, in view of later unemployment problems); large research grants were made; and many facilities were built. The scientific community was delighted with the money. University presidents rejoiced at NASA's boon.

At some point, however, the Webb perspective on SUP was lost. Webb grew unhappy with his middle-managers and finally replaced the director of the office charged with administering the program. The changes in middle-management made little difference in the results on campus, for the real barriers to society-oriented university research lay there, not in government.

The presidents of the universities had not responded to the obligation of the "Memorandum of Understanding" to seek new and more effective ways to make research results available and useful to external clienteles. During the Webb period, more than thirty-four memos had been signed, and at not one institution did Webb feel that "something happened." At some universities with strong traditions of basic research, the scientists were indifferent or hostile to such notions as Webb expounded. Other institutions cited compliance with the memorandum through advisory committees, conferences on applications of new findings, outside consulting relationships of individual faculty members, etc. Most of

29. *Ibid.,* p. 71.

this seemed trivial to Webb. He was seeking a more profound response: basic attitude changes, major restructuring on campus, and new external relationships for university personnel at all levels. Although he bombarded university presidents with letters and badgered them with visits, the university leaders (with one or two exceptions) did not accept Webb's vision. Either they never quite caught it, or if they did they could see no way to make it manifest except over very long periods of time. The built-in rigidities of the university were too great, and the resources at its disposal were too small, even with Webb's money.[30] SUP began with $4.6 million in 1962, peaked at $45.7 million in 1966, went down thereafter, and finally was phased out completely in 1971.

The program may have been too ambitious for the times. Webb wanted most to influence the top research universities, and the 1960's were so affluent for them that NASA had very little leverage. The other federal agencies diluted NASA's influence by continuing with project money and institutional grants in customary ways. These awards carried few, if any, of the strings of Webb's award. The universities liked SUP, but left its creator disillusioned by their lack of responsiveness to his society-oriented views. More importantly, the SUP record added to a general impression on the part of government as to the unresponsiveness of universities to societal needs. When former NASA "middle-managers" moved to NSF and other agencies in the 1970's, many took with them their negative views of universities, as experienced in SUP. Such attitudes weighed heavily against universities in the politics of science in the early 1970's.

Conclusion

The relationship of technoscience agencies to basic research has been discussed in this chapter. Various agencies have faced the same question: to whom or to what are they responsible? They are *public* organizations, but the work that they per-

30. *Ibid.*, p. 72.

form involves investments of the most uncertain kind in the public's long-range future. Over time, they may spend hundreds of millions, even billions—but, for what? The product is often intangible and incomprehensible to laymen. Most research agencies are supposedly instruments of broader public missions. The government does not support knowledge production on the scale it does just for the sake of the production of knowledge. The relationship of the research function to applied missions with societal goals is often obscure, however, both to those in the agencies and potential users. The relationship of basic research to users, other than the scientific community, may well be distant, but it is there. The research agency that forgets its user responsibility does so at its own peril. It is remarkable, therefore, that for many years some research agencies spun off, more or less out of the control of user interests and into the control of academic performers. That they did so provides ample evidence of the faith that the American people had in science at the end of World War II, and the capacity of research administrators to exploit that faith for the benefit of the scientific community. Historically, NIH and NSF certainly were more responsive to academic science than to any applied constituents. In the end, macropolitical pressures made their missions more applied.

James Webb used his NASA base to push a program that he believed would strengthen universities while they were being used to benefit NASA and the broader society. He built a multitude of space centers across the country. He called for interdisciplinary, problem-oriented research. He tried to make the most autonomous of R&D performer organizations more socially responsible. Still, evidences of success, at least on the scale that Webb demanded, were few and far between. With the coming of the 1970's there was a new environment for the universities, and the mood for what Webb wanted was more ripe. The society-oriented administrators of the 1970's conceived their role in much narrower terms than had Webb, however. They were prone to keep controls more in their own hands than to allow them to be exercised by university presidents. Webb sought societal emphasis *through* the institution. The society-oriented managers of the 1970's had little interest in institutions *per se*. Institutions, in fact, were regarded as a nuisance, an impediment to control over research and the researchers.

To what values and modes of research management should administrators, agencies, and universities adhere in the future? It is probable that, in previous years, there was too much of an attitude: what can government do for science? However, it is also true that there are equal dangers in leaning too far in the utilitarian direction. Without adequate protection, applied research can push out basic research in governmental settings as well as in business settings. Generally, applied science has more powerful constituents than does basic science. Society does have immediate needs. The scientific community and universities could be far more responsive than they are. On the other hand, there are invariably broader, longer-range questions that require fundamental research, where the maximum number of options must be explored if such problems are ever to be tackled successfully. Society-oriented administration is almost always *politically* ripe, but it may not always be technically ready. It is simpler to choose a target for research than to find a means to reach it.

How is it possible to get balance between society-oriented and science-oriented administration in one government agency, much less the technoscience agencies as a whole? How is it possible to get balance between funding for science projects and funding for universities as institutions? or between the scientific disciplines? or between large-scale and single-investigator science? It is clear that there are many conflicting interests to be weighed in the administration of basic research that are absent in the administration of applied research and development. Ultimately, however, they divide into values related to *policy for science* and those concerned with *science in policy*. The central questions of organizational design and governance involve how to represent, adequately and appropriately, these different perspectives in research administration. With too much power for applied interests, both basic science *and* ultimate solutions are likely to suffer. With too much control by the pure scientists, however, the government program is likely to be unresponsive to the legitimate interests and needs of the public-at-large. Finding the right balance may constitute the most complex and delicate of all problems in the governance of R&D.

7

Redirecting Science and Technology

THERE HAS BEEN a great deal of talk about redirecting or "re-deploying" science and technology from defense, space, and atomic energy—the traditional federal priorities—to other areas of national need.[1] Chapter 4 dealt with some aspects of reorientation from the perspective of technoscience agencies concerned with domestic/social areas, such as housing and urban mass transit. There were many bills introduced at the outset of the 1970's aimed at general redeployment, such as S.32 "The National Science Policy and Priorities Act of 1972," advocated by Senator Edward Kennedy. This authorized the expenditure of over $1 billion for several conversion programs and made parity of civilian and military R&D a matter of national policy.[2] These bills invariably failed

1. Redeployment is, of course, a constant process. It is seen most visibly when new policy arenas open up—space, environment, energy—and various agencies and R&D performers try to find a place in the new field, or at least to repackage their existing products in the language of the new field. Redeployment within an enlarging federal R&D budget is relatively easy. The problems come when the budget is not growing and the particular field with which an agency or lab is associated is losing favor.

2. Other legislative initiatives in this area have included: "The Economic Conversion Loan Authorization Bill" (S.1261; 92nd Cong.; 1st Sess.; Sen. Kennedy); "The National Economic Conversion Act" (S.4430; 91st Cong.; 2nd Sess.; Sen. McGovern); "The National Peacetime Transition Act of 1971" (S.1191; 92nd Cong.; 1st Sess.; Sen. McGovern); and "The Conversion Research and Education Act of 1971" (H.R.34; 92nd Cong.; 1st Sess.; Reps. Giaimo and Davis). For an analysis of much of this proposed legislation, see Ellis R.

to become law. Change has occurred more incrementally, with traditional areas of support remaining static or declining as new fields received increased federal spending. In the process of change many R&D performers have had to suffer drastic cutbacks in personnel as existing contracts ended and new ones failed to materialize.

Previous chapters have discussed technoscience agencies primarily in their roles as R&D sponsors. Of course, they are much more complex. Their sphere of influence encompasses performers as well, both directly through their own labs and indirectly through contracts to outside organizations. To re-direct R&D requires more than redeploying the headquarters level of technoscience agencies. It necessitates changing the performer institutions where the work of science and technology is ultimately done.

Among performer institutions, universities and industry have relative autonomy and freedom from control by the agencies. They can redeploy to new sponsors as national priorities change.[3] Federal labs, whether civil service or contractor-operated, are more closely linked to specific federal agencies and, therefore, have special problems in reorienting.[4] They are part of technoscience agencies—yet they are *apart from* these organizations. They are dominated by the scientific/technological estates and have their own institutional goals and identities. They are also at the bottom of a federal hierarchy that stretches upward to a specific federal sponsor

---

Mottur, *Conversion of Scientific and Technical Resources: Economic Challenge—Social Opportunity* (Washington, D.C.: Program of Policy Studies in Science and Technology, George Washington University, March 1971).

3. Universities and industry, on the other hand, may resist redeployment to new missions, as the NASA experience with universities illustrates. See Chapter 6 above.

4. There are many laboratories that are federally funded R&D centers (FFRDC's). They receive a sum of money from an agency sponsor every year on a regularized basis, just as do civil service labs. The difference is that they are nominally "private." Often, government owns the laboratory facilities, but the lab is operated on behalf of government by a private contractor. All of the atomic energy labs are FFRDC's. For our purposes, both civil service and FFRDC installations are treated as federal laboratories.

on whom they are dependent for financial survival. Thus, they are the technical core of mission-oriented R&D. They are "field" in a new variation on an old public administration theme: headquarters-field relations. For them to redeploy, or be redeployed, in a way that is independent of the sponsor, is to do more than move from one mission to another; it is to transfer allegiance from one federal agency to another. The existing sponsor may resist losing a resource. The new sponsor may not relish the prospect of continuing financial responsibility for a federal laboratory. It may fear divided loyalty on the part of the lab. Thus, it is much easier to talk about redirecting R&D than it is to accomplish such a feat. To redeploy R&D involves moving big scientific and technological organizations from one policy sector to another.

In the absence of a general policy for redeploying R&D, change does take place, but it is piecemeal. It occurs through the adjustments that a variety of performer and sponsor organizations make to the initiatives of one another. The interactions at this subsystem level are influenced, in turn, by the fractionated national policies occurring in their environment. Such national actions may help or hinder redeployment. A key factor in all cases is power: the power of old sponsors to retain their performer resources; the power of new sponsors to accept or resist the redeployment overtures of either the performers or their political allies; and the power of performer institutions themselves to control their own destiny. Federal labs, while the most public of all R&D performers, may have the greatest difficulty in adapting to shifts in national priorities. They are at the bottom of an administrative hierarchy. To whom or to what are they responsible? Are they agency labs or national labs? Who is to say? Between a lab and national policy is administrative policy. In the long run, administrative policy, as defined by old and new agency sponsors, may have more influence over redeploying R&D than the wishes of the labs or the needs of the nation.

Redeploying R&D implies change, both for performers and

sponsors—old and new. How is such change brought about or limited? Examined in this chapter will be three strategies for redirecting R&D at the "working," or laboratory, level. The focus of attention will be federal labs, but the strategies are applicable (with modifications) to other performer institutions. Each strategy differs in terms of the degree of change demanded on the part of the agencies and the performers. Each has a different locus of control on the pace and direction of redeployment. These strategies are: technology transfer, conversion, and diversification.

TECHNOLOGY TRANSFER

Technology transfer may be defined as the movement of technology developed in one institutional setting to an alternative use in a second institutional setting.[5] What this means in the redeployment context of high-technology agencies and laboratories is a commitment by technoscience agencies to seek to identify spin-offs from defense, space, or atomic energy R&D that may contribute to solving problems in secondary areas of application, such as biomedical or state and local public-service fields. Operating optimally from the agency's point of view, technology transfer would require little or no shifting of personnel or money from the main product-line activity, merely a shift of information and perhaps some hardware. All that would be needed to get technology "off the shelf" would be to alert a potential user to the availability of the technology through information dissemination techniques.

As a reorientation strategy, technology transfer has certain advantages from a sponsor's standpoint. It permits the sponsor to keep its lab directed to the mission of the agency. There is no need to involve additional sponsors, since the R&D has presumably already been accomplished. It is not an R&D

5. Samuel I. Doctors, *The Role of Federal Agencies in Technology Transfer* (Cambridge: MIT Press, 1969), p. 3.

capability *per se* that is thus redeployed, but the technology resulting as "spin-off" from R&D previously performed. While maintaining control over its lab, the agency can also reap some political benefit from the appearance of redeployment to new national priorities. Costs for the agency and taxpayers are minimized; so, of course, is genuine reorientation. If technology transfer had worked as well as its proponents had hoped it would, there would have been less need for alternative redeployment strategies. All would have gained from such a successful transfer strategy. But it usually does not work that well. In fact, a National Academy of Engineering study found the technology transfer record of the federal government to be exceedingly disappointing.[6] Whether technology transfer achieved the agencies' other goals of maintaining control over their labs while achieving a measure of political credit for redeployment, is another matter.

The growing realization of the inadequacies of technology transfer is revealed in the successive tactics used by NASA in its own spin-offs program. The space agency initiated its technology transfer program in 1962. The primary technique used to transmit NASA technology from its performers was the issuance of technical briefs, from various information centers located around the country, to a large sample of potential users. In the mid-1960's, when it became clear that these rather *passive* information dissemination tactics were not accomplishing very much, the agency added a much more aggressive marketing approach. Into the NASA technology transfer effort came *active* technology agents—government and contractor personnel. They would systematically search

6. National Academy of Engineering, *Technology Transfer and Utilization*. Report to the National Science Foundation (Washington, D.C.: National Academy of Engineering, 1974). A broader study by the author and Albert H. Teich found a similar record. See W. Henry Lambright and Albert H. Teich, *Federal Laboratories and Technology Transfer: Institutions, Linkages, and Processes*. Report to National Science Foundation (Syracuse and Binghamton, New York: Syracuse University Research Corporation and the State University of New York at Binghamton, March 1974).

the labs for transferable items that could be matched with urban and other non-space, public-service needs. Eventually, this approach led NASA to help start Public Technology, Inc. (PTI), an independent technology transfer service for state and local government. PTI looks for useful technology wherever it may be found, but the NASA ties remain strong. Some of the organization's top executives "transferred" from NASA.

These search/marketing techniques and linkage mechanisms still did not redirect much NASA technology. What became clear to NASA in the early 1970's was what the Agency for International Development had previously discovered in respect to the transfer of U.S. technology to less-developed countries: namely, that a great deal of high technology is inappropriate in the alternative institutional setting (e.g., fire-resistant clothing suitable for astronauts may be "over-engineered" and too expensive for local firemen). The consequence of this realization of the need for better technological "fit" was a further shift in NASA redeployment tactics. Now NASA began to adapt (product engineer) the technology to different user needs before transferring it.

Adaptive engineering is a form of user-oriented, user-defined R&D that NASA had not encouraged in the 1960's. In fact, lab personnel had been discouraged from engaging in tasks beyond the NASA mission, and at least one Jet Propulsion Laboratory researcher had been fired, in part for being too technology-transfer conscious. In the 1970's NASA relented, in line with a new emphasis on applications. Top NASA management was hardly enthusiastic about this particular spin-offs approach. The more the labs moved into an adaptive engineering mode, the more they engaged in R&D for others at NASA's expense. Did the political credit justify the costs? Technology might better be transferred under the new policy, but, in the process, the allegiance of the labs to the NASA space mission might be weakened. It is no wonder that most agencies have continued to emphasize information dissemination as a technology-transfer tactic. Such a method provides the symbol of redeployment while minimizing the bureaucratic risks of real change.[7]

CONVERSION

Redirecting R&D from one sponsor to another through the conversion of a facility is a strategy requiring the maximum of change for all parties to redeployment. Who is in charge of the process? Few (if any) labs deliberately choose to convert, not only because of the massive disruption in employee routines and established bureaucratic relationships that are involved, but also because of the loss of jobs. Agencies seldom like to lose a lab completely, and even new sponsors may not be particularly enthusiastic about gaining certain labs. The demand of the new sponsor agency may well be the controlling element, in terms of the *pace* of conversion, but it is too much to say that the new sponsor controls the redeployment process in conversion. Conversion is usually an inadvertent consequence of other national policy decisions. This can be seen by referring to two of the more important conversions of recent years: Fort Detrick and the Electronics Research Center (ERC). For Fort Detrick, the move was from germ warfare for the Army to cancer research for NIH. For ERC, the conversion took it from space research for NASA to transportation systems work for the Department of Transportation (DOT).

For both Fort Detrick and ERC the decision to convert was triggered by events outside their control. The Detrick decision was the result of a Presidential edict, announced November 25, 1969, to terminate all biological warfare research in the U.S. For Detrick, conversion thus began in the wake of technology arrestment. In the case of ERC, the decision also came from above, but it was more directly aimed at terminating ERC. NASA's budget was so cut by the Nixon administra-

7. National Academy of Engineering, *Technology Transfer, op. cit.*, p. i., reported that, of the $17 billion that federal agencies spent on R&D in FY 1973, nearly $1 billion was used for dissemination of technical information, while only $43 million was spent to adapt technology to new purposes.

tion that, on December 29, 1969, NASA decided that it had to reduce its base of operations. ERC, the newest NASA lab, was just getting under way and could most easily be cut. "We are simply faced with the hard fact that NASA cannot afford to continue to invest as broadly in electronics research as we have in the past," NASA management stated at the time.[8]

Hence, for Detrick and ERC, the choice was to convert or die. The only way to survive was to redeploy completely, to change sponsors and, thus, missions. In the case of both labs, help in finding new sponsors came from outside allies. The chief outside allies were the congressional delegations from the states in which the two facilities were located: Fort Detrick was in Maryland, and ERC was in Massachusetts. Scientists at the White House level were also active on behalf of the two labs, since it was felt that both labs contained people and equipment that were too important as national resources to be lost. DOD and NASA also helped to lobby to save their former labs.

It was one matter to agree on conversion as a redeployment/survival strategy and another to consummate the policy. The difficulty was to find a new agency willing to support and use the converted facility. Here, the conversion experiences of the two labs began to diverge. The major difference was that, in the ERC case, there was not only a push from the lab and its outside proponents to find a home for it, but also a pull from an alternative agency.

John Volpe, the Secretary of Transportation during the first Nixon administration, was a former governor of Massachusetts. He was sensitive to the political and human ramifications of growing unemployment of high-technology personnel in his home state, and he was also interested in improving the in-house technical competence of DOT. Volpe had been talking about building a research center for transportation. Building such a center would cost a great deal more than taking on an existing facility. In addition, Volpe's Undersecretary of Transportation, James Beggs, had joined DOT from a previous executive position with NASA. He was familiar with the Electronics Research Center. ERC found him helpful in making its case to DOT for becoming a part of that agency.

Volpe "persuaded President Nixon that, while the doomed NASA facility and its staffing may not have been exactly what the Department of Transportation would have developed from scratch, the set-up was approximate enough that DOT could make good use of it."[9] However, Volpe had to take on the new facility without additional money. The Nixon administration intended to maintain the budget saving realized by the NASA decision to close the Electronics Research Center. Since the DOT budget had already been "put to bed" Volpe said that his department would "rearrange" its budget to allow for the changeover without new money. What this meant to the agencies of his department was: "Here is a new capability for you to use—*but* it doesn't come for free—it will be paid for the first year out of *your* budget."[10] Thus, in March 1970, scarcely three months following the announcement of ERC's closing, President Nixon declared that ERC would be converted to Transportation Systems Center (TSC).

The demand from an alternative sponsor was missing in the Fort Detrick conversion. There was plenty of lab lobbying—but decisions were slow to materialize and be implemented. The technocratic core of Detrick lay in microbiology, and the logical place to move a microbiological facility seemed to be to the National Institutes of Health, particularly its National Cancer Institute. What might be logical from the point of view of Detrick and its friends was not so obvious from the NIH/NCI perspective. Fort Detrick was huge. With

9. "DOT's Transportation Systems Center: Real-Time Research in Reality," *Transportation and Distribution Management,* July 1973, p. 16.

10. James C. Elms, Director of the Transportation Systems Center, speech: "From Space to Earth—A New Look in Cambridge" (Boston, Mass., July 14, 1970). Emphasis in original.

1800 employees, it was twice the size of ERC. Its former germ-warfare mission repelled many civilian scientists. The equipment, while excellent, was also exceedingly specialized. The major problem was Detrick's expense, however. It would cost $15 million a year to maintain the lab in the manner to which it had become accustomed under DOD. Would NIH/NCI regard Detrick as a good investment? Apparently, the new prospective sponsor was somewhat ambivalent.[11]

In June 1970 the Deputy Secretary of Defense reported what seemed to be an accord that the Detrick facilities would be transferred to the Department of Health, Education and Welfare, in line with an HEW request.[12] However, NIH/NCI, which would eventually have to support Fort Detrick, wanted additional funds for the new lab. In 1970 the Senate passed legislation that added $15 million to the budget of NIH to enable the agency to include Detrick without cutting existing programs. However, the money was deleted in conference. Some Senators balked because NIH had revealed no detailed plans for how it would use Detrick. Was NIH dragging its feet deliberately? Was it using Detrick for budgetary bargaining purposes with the Nixon administration and Congress? These questions proved academic once the national decision to wage an accelerated program against cancer was announced. Now NIH/NCI would be looking for ways to spend a great deal of new cancer money. In October 1971 President Nixon went to Fort Detrick to announce that the facility would become the focal point for the National Cancer Institute's war on cancer. He declared that scientists who worked at Detrick could henceforth devote themselves "toward saving life, rather than destroying life."[13]

11. See Phillip M. Boffey, "Fort Detrick: A Top Laboratory Is Threatened with Extinction," *Science*, Vol. 171, January 22, 1971.

12. Comptroller General of the United States, *Report to Congress: Problems Associated with Converting Defense Research Facilities to Meet Different Needs: The Case of Ft. Detrick* (Washington, D.C.: General Accounting Office, 1972).

13. Robert Semple, Jr., "Nixon Counting on Conversion of Military Facilities," *New York Times*, October 19, 1971.

Because Detrick was further converted—from a civil service center to a federal contract center—additional time was lost. It was not until June 1972 that NIH signed a contract with Litton Bionetics to manage the facility on its behalf. The facility was now renamed the Frederick Cancer Research Center. In contrast to the $15 million-a-year reported earlier as required to maintain the lab, the contract called for only $6.8 million for the first year. Small by DOD and Fort Detrick standards, this still constituted the largest single award in the history of NIH.[14]

In the cases of both Detrick and ERC, the conversion process had been bumpy, but obviously far more so for Detrick. ERC kept its director and thus had a measure of internal stability and leadership throughout the conversion process. The director of Detrick did not stay to watch Detrick become a very different organization from the one he had built. While many professionals, particularly the physicists, left ERC when it moved to DOT with its more pragmatic problems, a good number of the better engineering researchers were retained by DOT. On the other hand, Detrick suffered a massive turnover of top professionals. What NIH inherited from Detrick for its war on cancer was primarily a set of buildings, equipment, and grounds. As a strategy for redeployment, conversion would appear to require the maximum of leverage from national policy levels. In Detrick, particularly, that leverage was missing, and as a result change occurred in a highly undirected way. DOT filled the leadership vacuum in the ERC conversion, somewhat. DOT's key role seemed to turn mainly on the fortuitous circumstance of having Volpe and Beggs pulling on behalf of their department. DOT's initiative gained Presidential and Office of Management and Budget backing. In the case of Detrick, no one came close to being in charge.

---

14. Harold Schmeck, Jr., "Litton To Run Cancer Research Lab," *New York Times,* June 25, 1972, p. 24.

DIVERSIFICATION

Minimal redeployment is seen in technology transfer (spin-offs). Maximum redeployment occurs in the case of conversion. Control over the redeployment process vests primarily with the traditional sponsor in transfer. Where control exists in conversion, it lies mainly with the new sponsor. Change for the involved parties is slight in transfer. It is quite significant in conversion, perhaps drastically so in the case of the R&D resource being converted. Hence, diversification is an intermediate strategy in many respects. There is redeployment, but the traditional sponsor does not lose its lab. The new sponsor gains the portions of a lab that it wants, but not an entire facility that it may not desire. The lab maximizes its control over its own future. In diversification, the moving force is usually found at the level of laboratory leadership. How does a lab steer a course for change when, in an agency's scheme of affairs, it is quite low in the administrative hierarchy?

Perhaps the best lessons are provided by Oak Ridge National Laboratory (ORNL) during the period 1955-73.[15] In this period ORNL reoriented itself to the extent that it went from a point where virtually all of its work was for the Atomic Energy Commission (AEC) to one where nearly 20 percent was for other agencies. The process went through stages which often characterize major organizational changes: a sense of threat from the environment, trigger for action, search for solutions, decisions, implementation, and routinization of the changes brought about.

THREAT FROM THE ENVIRONMENT

The redeployment of ORNL began with the sense of threat from the environment. The threat facing ORNL was per-

15. This section is based on current research on the diversification of federal laboratories under NSF sponsorship, by the author and Albert H. Teich. ORNL is a federally funded R&D center, operated on behalf of the government by Union Carbide Corporation.

ceived by Alvin Weinberg, who became director in 1955, having risen through the ranks from a bench scientist during the Manhattan project. In view of the milestone Atomic Energy Act of 1954, the emphasis in AEC was shifting from developing technology to deploying technology. There would be fewer large-scale atomic R&D projects and more competition for the work—both from other AEC labs and private manufacturers. In one of his first speeches as director, Weinberg speculated that, in time, ORNL might work itself out of a mission. He believed ORNL constituted a magnificent technoscience capability that should not be allowed to atrophy. He regarded ORNL as a national resource that should move with the nation's problems and not be held solely to AEC's mission. In other words, Weinberg sensed problems and potential new opportunities for ORNL and was preparing his institution for the necessity for change.

TRIGGER FOR ACTION

To go from a hazy sense of threat and potential opportunity to action required a trigger. That catalyst came in 1961, when two major R&D projects with which ORNL was heavily engaged were cancelled. These were the nuclear plane and the homogeneous nuclear reactor. At one point, 25 percent of ORNL's work force had been involved in the nuclear airplane project. These terminations were tangible evidence that, unless the lab diversified, it would face a future of anxiety and institutional shrinkage. At another level in the organization, the Biology Division, which had performed pioneering work for AEC in radiation-impact research, was under a threat of its own, unrelated to the big technology projects that dominated the lab as-a-whole. Biology was aware that, over the rest of the decade, AEC projected little growth in spending for the radiation biology work it had been doing. If the Biology Division wished to grow, it would have to look beyond AEC for support.

SEARCH FOR SOLUTIONS

There followed a search for alternative work from other government agencies. The leaders in this search were Weinberg, for the lab in general, and Alexander Hollaender, director of the Biology Division for that entity. The search was carried out at a variety of levels. Within the laboratory, a series of Advanced Technology Seminars were organized. ORNL's top management met and discussed the lab's capabilities and the emerging national R&D opportunities to which those capabilities might be applied. Hollaender was active in talking with friends and professional acquaintances in NIH. Weinberg worked at an even higher level. From 1959 to 1962 he was a member of the President's Science Advisory Committee (PSAC). Moreover, under the Kennedy administration many scientist administrators whom he knew well were moving into key positions of national leadership. These included: Jerome Wiesner, Kennedy's science adviser; Glenn Seaborg, the chairman of AEC; and Roger Revelle, the science adviser to the Secretary of the Interior. These professional ties allowed Weinberg to bypass normal bureaucratic channels—especially the career technocrats in AEC who might have questioned ORNL's entrepreneurial spirit.

DECISIONS

Weinberg's criteria for new ORNL projects were that they be "big, expensive, strongly in the national interest, and . . . not be ready for commercial exploitation."[16] Four of the most important diversification decisions made by ORNL during the 1960's took the lab into the areas of desalting, cancer, civil defense, and environment. The first three of these diversifications were undertaken in rapid succession, from 1962 to 1964. The environmental diversification did not occur until 1970.

16. Alvin M. Weinberg, "Problem of Missions," speech before the Institute for Scientists in Research and Development Laboratories (Washington, D.C.: The Brookings Institution, March 20, 1961).

ORNL's tactics in the early diversifications were to move quickly, using Weinberg's top-level contacts to smooth the necessary interagency negotiations. With Chairman Seaborg as a Weinberg ally, AEC found itself legitimating ORNL *faits accomplis.* ORNL presented each diversification as an ad hoc decision, fully justifiable in its own right, rather than as part of a general laboratory strategy for broadening the base of sponsor support.[17] As long as the issue of ORNL allegiance to AEC could be avoided—and Weinberg took special pains to underline that loyalty at every occasion—resistance at the administrative level was held in check. It was only in the late 1960's, when ORNL sought to diversify into environmental R&D, that problems arose in this regard.

The chief problem was the attitude of the Joint Committee on Atomic Energy toward ORNL's diversification. Diversification was fine with the JCAE, as long as it perceived it had lost nothing and had the potential for enlarging its jurisdictional domain through the initiatives of ORNL. When it sensed a possible redeployment outside of its control, it took umbrage. This happened in the case of environment. In the late 1960's, while policy for environment was still fluid (before there was an Environmental Protection Agency), Senators Muskie and Baker proposed a major R&D attack on environmental problems, with a system of environmental labs at its base. ORNL drew up a plan for the Senators that appeared to place ORNL as the "model" environmental lab. JCAE Chairman Chet Holifield had recently amended AEC statutes to permit laboratory diversification into environment, but he did not intend what he perceived as happening. On hearing of the ORNL move he was furious and reportedly exclaimed, "If Muskie wants a lab, he should get one of his own rather than try to take one from AEC."

In the 1970 AEC authorization bill, ORNL was excoriated. The JCAE chastised ORNL (without mentioning its name)

17. Harold Orlans, *Contracting for Atoms* (Washington, D.C.: The Brookings Institution, 1967), pp. 113–14.

for "empire building" and charged "one laboratory" with
soliciting "activities unrelated to its atomic energy programs
and for which it does not now have special competence or
talents." It admonished AEC and its national labs "to stay
within the bounds" of legislative intent. AEC immediately
followed this with strong guidelines geared to restricting
ORNL diversification.[18] In the end, ORNL did manage to
diversify into environment, but on a more modest scale than
originally contemplated and under NSF funding.

IMPLEMENTATION

There was a mixture of both the idealist and the realist in
Weinberg. He could speak the language of bureaucratic survival while, at the same time, expressing a true believer's faith
in the power of technology to "fix" public problems. He con-
tinually spoke of a "coherent" research program at the laboratory level that could synthesize what was fragmented at the
bureaucratic level. This was an argument that, by devolving
control of R&D to the lab level, the politics that surrounded
science and technology in Washington could somehow be ex-
cised. Whether or not Weinberg really believed this, the fact
was that politics was inseparable from ORNL diversification.
As the environment instance suggested, AEC and JCAE were
not naïve. At the lab level, what might have been primarily a
means for keeping all employees at work was, at the subsystem level, a possible way to expand jurisdictions. This was
understood by the new sponsors of ORNL—if perhaps not
fully appreciated by ORNL itself.

Desalting pointed up the problem. The desalting program
began via an end-run by ORNL around not only the career
technocrats of AEC but also the new sponsor, the Office of
Saline Water (OSW) in the Department of Interior. OSW was
informed by its departmental superiors that it was to fund a
desalting R&D program at ORNL. The lab was many times

18. David J. Rose, "New Laboratories For Old," *Daedalus,* Summer 1974,
Vol. 103, pp. 145-46.

the size of OSW, and the small, politically insecure agency feared that the performer tail would wag the sponsor dog. Worse, there was the potential bureaucratic rival, AEC, hovering in the background. The concern of OSW was justifiable. Shortly after the water research program was under way, AEC joined OSW in launching a new companion program that linked nuclear reactors to desalting. This particular program had great support in the White House. From it emerged the idea of combining nuclear reactors and desalting techniques to form giant "nuplexes" and "agro-industrial complexes" that would be deployed to help develop many poor, arid nations of the world. What diversification there was at the lab level could thus easily be seen by OSW as AEC imperialism at the bureaucratic level. Such developments caused OSW to tighten already strong administrative controls over that part of the program it could most influence: the original diversification effort of non-nuclear water desalting research.

Control was the issue. Relations between ORNL and OSW grew increasingly strained throughout the 1960's. The coherence Weinberg extolled was opposed by OSW. That agency divided the research effort into small segments, which its program managers could supervise, rather than provide a single, sizable chunk of money to Weinberg for *his* management. These were some of the problems of implementing diversification in desalting, and, in varying degrees, they were present in all other efforts. The bureaucratic politics of R&D reached down to the technical levels of the lab. ORNL's own ambitions, while couched in ideals and technical jargon, inevitably were rooted in a desire to survive, grow, and serve important needs. The new sponsors knew it and sought to use ORNL, rather than being used for the lab's—and AEC/JCAE's—aggrandizement.

ROUTINIZATION

With all of the problems in implementation and control among the various parties to ORNL diversification, the programs that were established ran their course and often led to additional efforts. Thus, civil defense got ORNL interested in cities. Social scientists were recruited, and, eventually, ORNL was under contract to HUD for other work. Ironically, one diversification option that ORNL did not follow until the 1970's was that of non-nuclear energy sources. Weinberg had broached the possibility as early as 1955. It had been discussed during the Advanced Technology Seminars, but, apparently, this was one area where ORNL could not move, perhaps because it suggested an AEC lab working in behalf of a source of energy that was competitive to the atom. Also, there was very little money around for non-nuclear energy R&D until 1973. The Arab oil crisis and subsequent broadening of AEC into ERDA removed this constraint at the lab level.

By the time Weinberg left ORNL for a post as chief of R&D for the Federal Energy Office, in 1973, diversification had become a program unto itself in ORNL and was regarded as such by AEC. Called "work-for-others," it had its own SOP's, "seed money," and even an administrative officer. What had begun and had been justified at first as a series of ad hoc specific efforts, had become part of the official expectations of AEC and its labs in the early 1970's. "Work-for-others" stood at approximately 20 percent of the overall lab effort. This amount was not insignificant in a $100 million-plus operation such as ORNL. An organizational innovation had become a bureaucratic routine and, presumably, would continue under ERDA.

CONCLUSION

Missing in redeployment is a systematic national policy that considers science and technology resources.[19] This can be seen

19. As in many areas, the House Subcommittee, chaired in the 1960's by Emilio Daddario, pioneered in attempting to draw attention to this important and usually neglected need in science and technology policy. See U.S. Congress House Committee on Science and Astronautics, Subcommittee on Science, Research, and Development. *Hearings, Utilization of Federal Laboratories,* 90th Cong., 2nd Sess. (Washington, D.C.: USGPO, 1968).

by looking beneath the rhetoric about "redirecting" science and technology to the manner in which such redirection takes place—largely in the *absence* of any coherent national policy. The vacuum in national policy is best illustrated by the redeployment or non-redeployment of federal labs—the keystone of technoscience agency R&D performing institutions. No R&D institutions are closer to government policy and administration. They are established and maintained in order that they may serve the missions of their sponsor agencies.

Missions wax and wane in national importance. When a mission loses priority, should the lab that has served that mission be allowed to wither, or should it be terminated? Should problem-oriented R&D institutions be encouraged to find new sponsors and new problems? At present, there is no policy, save for what occurs ad hoc through the negotiations among labs and traditional and new sponsors. Whether R&D labs redeploy through technology transfer or conversion or diversification techniques, they tend to do so in a national-policy void. As a consequence, technology is not transferred; labs are "converted" but professional talent is lost; and diversification proceeds, for better or worse, mostly in accord with the bureaucratic political talents of a given lab director.

8

Governing Science and Technology

WHO GOVERNS federal science and technology? What is national R&D policy? Who makes it? How adaptive is the R&D system to changing national needs?

In approaching questions such as these, this book has focused on the large-scale R&D-intensive operating agencies: NASA, AEC/ERDA, NIH, DOD, NSF, etc. These have been called the technoscience agencies. Here is where policy purpose must be united with administrative means; where what the politicians *want* done must be meshed with what the scientists and engineers *can* do; where considerations of scientific research, technological development, and utilization must all be merged with political feasibility and public acceptance. Such agencies and departments are not only at the heart of America's R&D administrative system, they can be found also at the beginning, middle, and end of federal science and technology policy.

This concluding chapter will review the nature of federal science and technology policy; review the role of the technoscience agencies and departments in its formulation and implementation; and discuss the problem of whether these administrative organizations are tools or masters in their relationship with national policy.

NATIONAL POLICY AND SCIENCE AND TECHNOLOGY

Is there a national science and technology policy? There is certainly no general, overarching, long-range course-setting for the federal government-as-a-whole in R&D affairs. That kind of policy does not exist. What constitutes the reality of policy is more a combination of initiatives, mostly from the agencies, but occasionally from central political authority. This sum-of-the-parts policy may be called *de facto* to distinguish it from more *strategic* approaches. To examine this *de facto* policy, it is useful to distinguish science from technology. It can be said that there has been a *de facto* national science policy, and there has been a *de facto* national technological development policy.

SCIENCE

The United States had one *de facto* national science policy for approximately two decades, from the end of World War II to approximately 1967. It is now in the process of institutionalizing a quite different national science policy. The original policy rested, according to Orlans, on these major assumptions:

1. Expenditures for basic research should increase markedly;
2. The output of Ph.D.'s should also be greatly increased;
3. Whenever possible, government-sponsored basic research should be conducted on campus because of the mutually beneficial relationship between research and education.[1]

An additional four assumptions underlying this policy might be added, all of which pertain to the notion that sci-

1. Harold Orlans, "Developments in Government Policies Toward Science and Technology," in Albert H. Rosenthal, ed., *Public Science Policy and Administration* (Albuquerque: University of New Mexico Press, 1973). Reprinted, *Brookings Reprint 274* (Washington, D.C.: The Brookings Institution, 1973), p. 228.

ence policy should be made and administered in the interests
of scientists:

1. The administration of basic research should respect scientists' freedom and minimize accountability procedures;
2. Money should flow through many agencies, rather than
   one central science support organization, in order to
   maximize the opportunity of a proposal for receiving
   support;
3. The best scientists at the best universities should be
   supported, but that money should also flow to build new
   "centers of excellence"; and
4. Peer review methods should determine which basic science proposals should receive support.

Together, these assumptions undergirded the policies to
which the administrative agencies adhered for many years.
Easily, the most important single dimension of that policy
was that of *growth* in federal support for science. Growth
made all other aspects possible. At the peak of growth in the
mid-1960's, leading academic scientific spokesmen called for
what was, in effect, a guaranteed annual increment of 15 percent to the federal budget for basic science. At that time, scientific expenditures had been growing at a commensurate
rate. They embodied the policy assumptions noted earlier.
What the scientists wanted was more insurance against a potential change in policy than the initiation of a new policy.
They wanted a *de jure* national policy in place of the *de facto*
one then in existence.

Orlans reports that the 15 percent per year proposal

. . . was accepted as the Johnson Administration's official target
for fiscal years 1966 and 1967. However, under the mounting demands of our two-front war in Vietnam and urban America,
HEW Secretary John Gardner challenged the wisdom of that
policy in the summer of 1966 and the following spring even the

President's science advisor Donald Hornig was admonishing his fellow scientists that though 'we [that is, the administration] accept . . . that America must be second to none in most of the significant fields of science [which he carefully did not enumerate] . . . what is *not* accepted is the notion that every part of science should grow at some automatic and predetermined rate, 15 percent per year or any other number. . . .'[2]

In retrospect, the claim for 15 percent per year for basic science may seem incredible. At the time it was not, however, for what was requested was simply a formalization of what was already an informal policy. Obviously, such growth could not continue, and, when science spending leveled off, all the other assumptions began fading. After a few years of transition, it would appear that the "new" national science policy, as *de facto* as its predecessor, rests on the following tenets:

1. The federal government must support basic academic research, since the market system will generally not do so. However, the federal government should establish priority areas that relate to explicit national needs.
2. The output of science and engineering Ph.D.'s has produced a sufficient number, in terms of most areas of national R&D needs, and should be stimulated by federal policy only in exceptional cases.
3. Universities cannot be privileged in the "institutional choices" of federal science policy. For scientific research of a large-scale, interdisciplinary, problem-oriented kind, particularly where deadlines in delivery of research "products" are involved, other research institutions may be more useful to government than are universities.
4. Basic researchers must be made more "accountable" for the spending of public funds.
5. The mission agencies should sponsor research that serves their mission rather than that of the universities, and

2. Cited by Orlans, *ibid.*, pp. 229–30.

NSF should play a larger role (and DOD a lesser) in overall federal support of academic research.

6. The market test should determine which scientists and universities get awards; money is too scarce to permit "institutional" grants for have-nots unless the grants relate to certain other national objectives (e.g., upgrading predominantly black universities and colleges in science and technology).

7. Peer review must be tempered more by management perspectives of government. The relevance of a proposal to an agency program is more important than its intellectual rigor or "eminent" principal investigator.

This new policy is not "anti-science" as much as it is indicative of the governmental desire to spend scarce resources in accord with near-term political, rather than longer-term scientific priorities. Whether better or worse as policy, it is certainly different from that which went before. Science policy has become more "society-oriented." As administered, however, it may violate many scientific norms, work against the interests of universities as research institutions, and bring to basic research a "management" perspective that, if pushed too far, may be unrealistic and even harmful to governmental, as well as scientific, purposes.

TECHNOLOGY

To speak of a technology policy would have been unusual prior to 1970. It is a mark of change that what was once called "science policy" has increasingly become "science and technology policy," and there are those who speak only of "technology policy." The new vocabulary reflects not only the relative fall of the scientific estate and of the university from political esteem over the years, but also the increasing interest in technology (if not in technologists) because of negative consequences of technology as well as—paradoxically—the need for quick solutions by means of technology.

What makes technology problematic for analysis also provides it strength in the policy process. Technology is so much a part of society's missions that it becomes difficult to know where a technology policy ends and a military, environmental, or transportation policy begins. The boundaries of federal development have been used in the present study to encompass technology policy. Included have been not only engineering development expenditures *per se* but also the applied research associated with development and attempts, through demonstrations and other incentives, to introduce federally funded technology to operational use. There is much more to federal technology policy than this, of course. The patent system, tax policy, and anti-trust statutes are all involved, but only *direct* efforts by government to stimulate technological innovation have been discussed here.

Interest in technology policy began building in the late 1960's and has continued to this day. New public policies and administrative institutions have been created to deal with various aspects of federal technology. Yet, like science policy in the narrow sense of basic research expenditures, technology policy has emerged, through no great edict from on high but rather through many small, day-to-day decisions occurring in a variety of places.[3]

Furthermore, behind technology policy stands no group as easily identifiable as the scientific community—amorphous as *that* group may be. The interests of "technologists" are melded into those of the institutions for which they work, whether governmental or industrial. The values of scientists tend to be more independent of the scientists' institutional affiliation, although the university is surely a congenial home.

The fact that a federally funded technological development policy is harder to identify and trace does not mean that one has not existed and has not undergone considerable redefini-

3. On such policy-making by incremental means, see Charles Lindblom, *The Intelligence of Democracy: Decision Making Through Mutual Adjustment* (New York: The Free Press, 1965).

tion in recent years. As with science, the watershed in *de facto* federal technology policy appears to have occurred during the late 1960's. The shift in emphasis can be stated as follows. The *former* technology policy assumed:

1. Federal development responsibilities center almost exclusively on defense, space, and atomic energy sectors, and massive expenditures in these areas primarily grow out of national security and international prestige needs;
2. Domestic technological development (aside from civilian nuclear power) is mainly the responsibility of the private sector or the states;
3. Federal development investment will indirectly benefit domestic technologies through "spin-offs" from defense and space technologies; and
4. Technological development aimed at economic growth is equivalent to "progress" and is inherently good.

The *new* technology policy assumes:

1. The three leading "national security" sectors of technological investment remain dominant, but not *as* dominant as they once were. This is particularly due to significant decreases in space technology spending since the mid-1960's and the relative growth of other domestic-oriented sectors. The concentration of development investment in defense, space, and atomic energy is seen to have diverted talent and federal money from other important concerns, such as those related to urban and economic development and non-nuclear energy sources.
2. Reliance on private market or state and local governments to fill the gaps in overall technological investment has not worked. The gaps have not been filled, leading to technological lag in certain sectors at home and balance-of-payments problems abroad.
3. The assumption that many domestic problems could be

solved through defense and space spin-offs has not been borne out by results. The federal government must, therefore, increase and in other ways seek to redirect various R&D performer institutions, many of which are underutilized in the three traditional fields of federal technological investment.

4. Technology may produce solutions, but it also produces problems, particularly for the environment. These should be thoroughly understood and, if possible, mitigated before launching and deploying new technologies.

The national technology policy has thus changed. The shift in national technology policy has reflected the broader turn in national priorities from national security/international prestige to domestic needs. As Bruce Smith points out:

In 1971, for the first time, the Health, Education and Welfare budget exceeded the Department of Defense budget and, although this was accomplished by some manipulation of figures, the expenditures for research and development for other than military purposes are becoming increasingly important. In all, defense, space, and foreign affairs expenditures, which a decade ago accounted for 53 percent of the federal budget, have shrunk to 34 percent in the fiscal year 1973. Social service expenditures increased from 27 to 43 percent of the federal budget during the same period.[4]

The shift in priorities, associated with the high hopes of Johnson's Great Society, was slowed by the war in Vietnam and the Nixon years. Nevertheless, a gradual change in spending patterns did take place. The agencies behind national security technologies remain the leading generators of development funds, but the domestic agencies have been advancing. The shift may not have occurred as fast as, or to the extent that some critics would like, but it has taken place.

4. Bruce L. R. Smith, "A New Science Policy in the United States," *Minerva*, Vol. 11, April 1973, p. 167.

Aside from the initial Great Society legislation which provided a catalyst for change, these alterations in priorities have occurred with only minimal Presidential leadership. For a while, during the Nixon administration, it appeared that such leadership would be forthcoming. As John Logsdon recounts:

In July 1971, the White House Domestic Council began an effort to identify "new technological opportunities" (N.T.O.) that were both related to national needs and at the same time would contribute to stimulating the economy. This review was perhaps the most intensive examination of the substance of, and rationale for, federal involvement in supporting non-defense research and development ever undertaken. . . .

The White House initiated the review of technological opportunities with the overly optimistic hope that such an analysis could (in the words of a Presidential message to Congress of September, 1971) "find the means to insure that . . . the remarkable technology that took . . . Americans to the moon can also be applied to reaching our goals here on earth." Those in charge of the N.T.O. study hoped to identify a few "domestic Apollo programs" with which Mr. Nixon could dramatize a new federal policy for technology.[5]

There was no trouble identifying "opportunities," and for a while, "White House officials were reported to have told representatives of industry that several billion dollars' worth of new research and development contracts might result from the effort."[6] However, when the New Technology Opportunities Program reached the President's inner circle of budgetary/political advisers, it was seriously deflated. "When it was finally presented in President Nixon's message on science and technology in March 1972—the first message by an American president dealing specifically with science and technology—

5. John Logsdon, "Toward a New Policy for Technology: The Outlines Emerge," *Technology Review,* October/November 1972, pp. 36–37.
6. Smith, *loc. cit.,* p. 169.

its magnitude had been greatly reduced. In fact, only $40 million in new funds were provided, to be used for investigation by NSF and the National Bureau of Standards into ways of accelerating technological innovation."[7] That ended the attempt to redirect technology efforts through topside planning. In his speech, the President called for "an overall strategic approach in the allocation of federal scientific and technological resources." By "strategic," the President meant a closer linking of federal research and development investment with national goals and priorities. Key elements of this approach were a determination better to apply "our scientific resources in meeting civilian needs" and to do so through "a new partnership in science and technology—one which brings together the federal government, private enterprise, state and local governments, and our universities and research centers in a coordinated, cooperative effort to serve the national interest."[8]

What the President said and what he did were not the same. The "strategic" approach was undermined by Nixon himself in early 1973, when he eliminated the Presidential science and technology machinery. The only opportunities seized were those that presented partisan political advantage, such as the Morgantown Personal Rapid Transit System. The expected acceleration in domestic R&D did not come. Urban mass transit innovation lagged. Operation Breakthrough petered out. It took the Arab energy crisis to speed up increased non-nuclear energy expenditures. The energy R&D build-up was in the mode of ad hoc, reactive, crisis decision-making—hardly in the strategic mode that Nixon had promised.

The emerging technology policy of the 1970's was not limited to issues of *stimulating* new technologies, however. There were also questions of *controlling* technology, as symbolized by the National Environmental Policy Act of 1969 and the creation of the congressional Office of Technology

7. *Ibid.*, pp. 169–70.
8. Logsdon, *loc. cit.*, p. 38.

Assessment in 1972. From the technoscience agencies' perspective, here were two new barriers to innovation. Technology assessment was, in fact, frequently equated by its opponents with technology "arrestment." Clearly, federal technology policy underwent significant changes in the 1970's, just as did federal science policy.

TECHNOSCIENCE AGENCIES AND POLICY MAKING

The role of technoscience agencies in the making of science and technology policy has been described well by William Carey, a former high-ranking official of the Office of Management and Budget, who later served as Chief Executive Officer of the American Association for the Advancement of Science. "We in the United States," Carey has stated, "have devolved great responsibility upon the mission agencies of the government for recognizing scientific opportunities, for sustaining the nation's research capabilities, for creating new scientific initiative, for determining where the public interest lies in matters of science and technology, for stewardship in seeing to the quality of publicly-supported research, and for anticipating emerging national problems and rates of social and technological change which call for long-range research strategies."[9]

How have the technoscience agencies performed their task? Administrative agencies exist in a forcefield of conflicting interests. They are pressed on all sides by the President and his Executive Office, Congress, courts, R&D performers, governmental and non-governmental users, the changing mood of the American people, and even foreign governments. In addition, there are the claims made by career officials who have their own stakes in what the agency does or does not do. From all these pressures and counter-pressures, an administrative

---

9. William Carey, "Science Policy-Making in the United States," in A. De Rueck, ed., *CIBA Foundation and Science of Science Foundation Symposium on Decision-Making in National Science Policy* (London: J. and H. Churchill, 1968), p. 143.

policy emerges to guide the agency in science and technology affairs. To grasp better the role of technoscience agency policy-making, it is useful again to separate a consideration of science policy from that of technology policy.

SCIENCE

There was a national debate on science policy from 1945 to 1950. It culminated in the establishment of the National Science Foundation (NSF). While this debate was going on, however, administrative science policy was already being forged. The dominant science-oriented agency, created in the immediate wake of World War II, was not NSF, the scientists' choice, but rather the Office of Naval Research (ONR). Who decided that the Navy should take the lead for the U.S. government in science policy? The moving force for creation was a group of young naval officers who called themselves the "Bird Dogs."[10] Seeing both a need, given the slowness of NSF to get authorized, and an opportunity, due to the desire on the part of the military to maintain ties with the scientific community, this bureaucratic interest group lobbied within the Navy and relevant congressional committees to get the necessary legislation passed for a program. What could not be done, directly, for five years—establishing an NSF—could be carried out, indirectly, through a mission agency (particularly a military agency) to which the politicians accorded much money and great discretion. Once in being, ONR won a distinguished academic clientele by providing sizable grants with few strings. While the Navy ran the program, it was most responsive to the scientific estate. The Navy paid the bill, but, from its perspective, the bill was very small.

The story of NIH was similar. Inheriting the biomedical contracts from OSRD at the end of the war, the National In-

10. "The Evolution of the Office of Naval Research," *Physics Today*, Vol. 14, August 1961, pp. 30–35. Cited in J. L. Penick, Jr. et al., *The Politics of American Science, 1939 to the Present* (Chicago: Rand McNally, 1965), pp. 132–37.

stitutes of Health (NIH), spurred by powerful allies, garnered additional legislation and began the process that produced the biomedical research empire seen today. Clearly a new "policy space" in basic science support had opened up following World War II, and, while Congress, the President, and the scientific community debated endlessly over the specifics of a national science policy of which NSF would be the cornerstone, various administrative entities and their congressional/interest-group allies moved quickly to establish beachheads, taking advantage of the postwar, pro-science national consensus. In some cases, the initiative came from administrative interest groups, as in the military services. In others, it came from non-governmental interest groups, as in the case of NIH. In each instance, science support was justified as instrumental to a practical mission rather than as a policy in and of itself. By the time NSF finally got under way, in 1951, it had to carve out a role amidst the ongoing programs of such agencies as ONR, AEC, and NIH. While national policy on science had lagged, administrative policy had moved ahead.

The Eisenhower administration, aware of the proliferation in basic science support, sought some controls on the enterprise in the interest of budgetary and organizational efficiency. One target of Presidential efforts at coordination was the Office of Scientific Research (OSR) in the Air Force. Unlike ONR, OSR had failed to obtain legislative legitimacy for its program prior to entering the federal science arena. Nick Komans notes that, in 1954, the Bureau of the Budget, acting on behalf of the President, decreed that the Air Force had neither the right nor the need to support basic academic research. In response, Komans relates, OSR's "budget was moved under a line item for the B-58. And, for all the Budget Bureau knew, the $4.7 million it approved was for research connected with the development of this aircraft, clearly within the realm of applied research. But, in reality, this money was handed over to the OSR to use, as originally planned, for basic research."[11]

Science policy by administrative agencies was given impetus with the birth of the National Aeronautics and Space Administration (NASA). NASA's major contribution in this field, the Sustaining University Program (SUP) of James Webb, had no specific legislative authorization at all. The program was off and running for two years before Congress debated its merits. Once again, science was justified as instrumental to the larger mission for which there was widespread public and, in this case, strong Presidential support. When various legislators, unfriendly to what they viewed as one more massive federal aid to higher education program, tried to kill SUP, the space committees rushed to NASA's defense. The Senate committee, in particular, held special hearings to provide *post facto* legitimacy.

Whatever was said or done at "the highest levels" of governance about science, the reality of policy was occurring at the administrative level. A plethora of "little NSF's"—in the aggregate *much* larger than the designated *National* Science Foundation—dominated federal science policy. As long as overall budgets were on the rise and the more general mood of the country was favorable to science and technology, there was little questioning of *de facto* national science policy— certainly not by the recipients of the funds of the various agencies. Only when a combination of circumstances occurred —the budget crunch of the late 1960's, Vietnam, problems of the cities, student riots on campus—did the clients discover there was another face to administrative pluralism.

In theory, the advantage of the decentralized approach to scientific support derived from the close coupling of research to mission. In fact, the "other" NSF's were science-oriented

11. Nick A. Komans, *Science and the Air Force, A History of the Air Force Office of Scientific Research* (Arlington, Va.: Historical Division, Office of Aerospace Research, 1966), p. 56. Cited by Daniel S. Greenberg, *The Politics of Pure Science* (New York: New American Library, 1967), p. 129.

not mission-oriented. When the larger environment changed, the science-oriented agencies and their clients found themselves going against the tide. With no strategic national policy for science, with science support over the years having been justified primarily in instrumental terms by mission agencies, the shift toward "relevance" left the science-oriented agencies and their performers with little in the way of protection. Not even going "underground," as the Air Force's Office of Scientific Research had done, sufficed when budget stringencies made it necessary for parent agencies and departments to make painful tradeoffs between service delivery, near-term technology, and long-term science. The dominant direction of NSF growth in the 1970's was applied.

Change came with a shock to most of the science-oriented agencies and their performer constituents. The slowness of these agencies to change rested on an unrealistic expectation that the "old" policies would last forever. Career people in the agencies, as well as their clients, had somehow become isolated from larger trends in society. The growth assumptions on which the programs were running were, in retrospect, bound to change. Once in motion, the administrative machinery seemingly could not be stopped or turned around. When change finally came, it ended some science-support programs, reorganized others, and left enormous dislocations and disruptions among the agencies and performers of basic science.

There had been warnings. As long before as 1958, speaking of basic research at universities, the aforementioned William Carey admonished the scientific community:

We must realize that, when science and education become instruments of public policy, pledging their fortunes to it, an unstable equilibrium is established. Public policy is, almost by definition, the most transient of phenomena, subject from beginning to end to the vagaries of political dynamism. The budget of a government, under the democratic process, is an expression of the objectives, aspirations, and social values of a people in a given webb of circumstances. To claim stability for such a product is to claim too much. In such a setting, science and education have become soldiers to fortune. Today their fortunes, happily, are in the ascendant.[12]

By the late 1960's those fortunes were in decline. Why did the technoscience agencies, which should have been sensitive to shifts in national policy, fail to adapt so as to minimize the damage to themselves and their scientific clients?

TECHNOLOGY

As administrative agencies have served as the locus for science policy over the years, they have done so also for technology policy. The "heartland" of federal technology policy has been dominated by a few agencies for many years. DOD, NASA, and AEC constituted the major spenders until 1974. The energy legislation of that year merely replaced AEC with an even larger R&D agency, Energy Research and Development Administration (ERDA). The actions of these major technoscience agencies have been geared to the development and deployment of technologies under their charge. Behind most large-scale technological systems that have been promoted in the military, space, and atomic energy fields have been huge administrative networks linking government, industry, and the university. These administrative systems have reached into congressional districts across the country. Big, high-technology development projects, once started, often become very difficult to stop. The longer they are in being, the greater are the stakes of those associated with them.

In the case of military technology, it sometimes has appeared that DOD has been unconsciously allied with its counterpart in the Soviet Union. Each has been engaged in a technological arms race against the other, with the diplomats

12. William Carey, "The Support of Scientific Research," *Scientific Man- power—1957: Papers of the Sixth Conference of Scientific Manpower* (Washington, D.C.: National Science Foundation, 1958), pp. 23–26. Cited in J. L. Penick, Jr. et al., *The Politics of American Science, 1939 to the Present, op. cit.*, p. 189.

and politicians of both countries having common problems in keeping the weapons R&D machinery under some semblance of restraint.

There have been similar problems where the national security elements of space and atomic energy were concerned. The AEC's civilian applications policy tended to be narrowly promotional. AEC proved overly protective and defensive with respect to the atom. It "repeatedly sought to suppress studies by its own scientists that found nuclear reactors were more dangerous than officially acknowledged or that raised questions about reactor safety devices."[13] NASA, similarly, was very slow to move its technological perspective from manned space flight and scientific probes of the planets toward greater attention to applications on earth. The space agency saw its budget virtually cut in half before it made significant internal changes in organization and priorities. Not until 1971 did NASA increase the visibility and bureaucratic influence of its Office of Applications. Prior to that, in funding and in organizational status, earth applications were third in agency priorities. NASA's congressional committees had been urging the agency to give more emphasis to earth-oriented work for years, but the agency had resisted. It had even discouraged efforts at diversification in that direction in some of its labs.

As NASA had been reluctant to admit the downturn of public interest in space exploration, particularly manned space flight, so AEC had been unwilling to respond to the environmental movement. It had to be jarred by the courts into realization that there was a new mood in the country. It was significant that the Joint Committee, rather than making the organization more cognizant of change in its political environment, had apparently itself become overly captivated by the atomic quest. Diversification of the national laboratories, led by Oak Ridge, preceded change at the AEC level. This

13. David Burnham, "AEC Files Show Effort To Conceal Safety Perils," *The New York Times,* Nov. 11, 1974, p. 1:1.

diversification was viewed with some ambivalence by AEC and the Joint Committee. Diversification was fine so long as the labs remembered that they were primarily *nuclear* labs. When one (Oak Ridge) flirted too seriously with the environment mission, it was rebuked. It took a crisis—induced by the Arabs in 1973-74—to provide the opportunity to broaden administrative policy. This was achieved under ERDA only by balancing non-nuclear vis-à-vis nuclear energy R&D and by splitting off the atom's regulators from the dominant promoters. Instead of anticipating or even being responsive to growing public concerns, a major technoscience agency, AEC, fought change and eventually found itself a victim of events.

It it clear that power in policy-making has been delegated to administrative agencies or has been seized by them. In some cases it is noteworthy that this power has led to creativity and initiative on the part of agencies. In others it has witnessed non-action, self-protection, resistance to change, or the favoring of external clienteles at the expense of the broader society. Given their important role in national science and technology policy, technoscience agencies cannot escape a share of blame for the turbulence experienced by the R&D system in recent years. In many cases the agencies did not foresee emerging national priorities and did not meet them. Where science and technology policies were at issue, it was business-as-usual for most of these agencies—and, thus, for the nation.

TECHNOSCIENCE AGENCIES: TOOLS OR MASTERS OF POLICY?

Théo Lefèvre, former Prime Minister of Belgium and a member of a group of foreign observers sent to study United States science policy by the Organisation for Economic Co-operation and Development, said in the group's 1968 report that the team had come to the United States "looking . . . for something which was not there: a science policy, distinct from general policy,[14] with its own aims and its special admin-

14. Lefèvre is including technology policy in his discussion of "science policy."

istration and programmes." Instead, he stated, what the visitors found was "a plurality of policies and responsibilities split between varied but nonetheless converging agencies." Such arrangements might work in the United States; however, "it is not, in our view, because of their intrinsic qualities, but in spite of defects which are no doubt tolerable and even profitable in a society of plenty, but which would be unacceptable in a European society with limited resources."[15]

The administrative machinery of federal R&D took its shape largely in the postwar period. What was "tolerable and even profitable" for many years may well be irrelevant or disastrous for the remainder of the century.

The problems that once gave a sense of national consensus, such as the "Soviet threat," have not been solved but have been joined by a host of additional troubles. Such difficulties now divide, more than unite, the country. Population, pollution, urban decay, poverty, the proliferation of nuclear weapons, a finite planet, and an ever-expanding demand for energy, food, and other resources—these are a beginning, but only a beginning, of a catalogue of great problems with which the United States and the world must deal. In the aftermath of Vietnam and Watergate, the nation faces them with less than traditional American confidence in its problem-solving capacity. Self-assured or not, however, the nation will have little choice but to try. These great problems will not vanish. They will become more and more serious.

Indicted as the cause of some woes, science and technology, nevertheless, are certain to be envisioned as solutions to whatever crisis must be attacked at a given moment. R&D may not provide the best answers for all problems. For instance, the perplexities of national security may be worsened by the creation of even more modern weapons. The more sophisticated the weapons and the greater their destructive potential, the greater is the fear and apprehension concerning their possible

15. Organisation for Economic Co-operation and Development, *Reviews of National Science Policy: United States* (Paris: OECD, 1968), pp. 360–61.

deployment and use. In the absence of other solutions, however, or in conjunction with them, technological fixes are likely to be major factors in national policy in the future, as they are today and have been in the past. Science and technology have become constants in federal decision-making, even with the decreases and other uncertainties of funding in recent years. The issue is not *whether* science and technology will be utilized but in what direction to place their capability—for whose benefit? for whose harm?[16] That course-setting should depend on national R&D policy.

DE FACTO POLICY

Who makes policy depends greatly on how the nation organizes itself with respect to a given function.[17] Organization biases a policy-making process in certain directions. It provides some actors privileged positions to influence what is done and how it is done. The more centralized a function is, the more the policy is determined by individuals and groups at the top. The more decentralized a function is, the more the policy is made at a lower level. The American R&D policy-making system was centralized during World War II and has been decentralized since then. This being the case, national policy has most often emerged from the technoscience agencies. This middle-level of policy-making has interacted, day by day, with the technical community and key legislators and committee staff. National policy there has been, but it has been, for the most part, *de facto* legitimations of decisions made below.

De facto national policy has certain characteristics. It tends to be pluralist in base and incrementalist in approach. It is this way because the policy process is structured to suit the needs of technoscience agencies—*existing* agencies. Techno-

16. Also, a major danger is that political leaders will use science and technology as palliatives and means to *avoid* trying to deal with underlying social problems.

17. See Harold Seidman, *Politics, Position, and Power: The Dynamics of Federal Organization,* 2nd edition (New York: Oxford University Press, 1975).

science agencies make policy by extending their present position to the next year, at slightly more cost. They take the next step in a "policy space." They make the initial and—under decentralized policy procedures—usually determinative trade-offs. Within the R&D structure, for example, these trade-offs may be between basic research on the one hand and applied research and development on the other. More broadly, there are also trade-offs between R&D expenditures, generally, and oprational programs.[18]

Technoscience agencies decide which science and technology programs to support and their relative priorities. They influence the pace of technology development and the timing of deployment. Higher authority may reject, delay, question, or even change administrative policy, but it usually begins where the agencies leave off. Technical, programmatic judgments and advocacy start at the administrative levels. These technical, programmatic judgments, however, are the crux of policy in R&D. These "small" decisions aggregate into the big decisions that set the course of overall government. Thus, when money is tight, science and technology must be linked very closely to agency goals as the price of survival. This may be desirable, up to a point, in making for a better connection between the products of an R&D program and the wants of sponsors and users. Invariably, however, the longer-range needs are slighted in the process.

Moreover, the pluralist, incrementalist, decentralized approach to R&D policy has an overriding defect. By giving major responsibility for planning in science and technology to the agencies and departments, it allows *plans* to grow out of agency goals. Most of these will relate to *programs* the agency wants. The agency invariably hopes its *plans* will become national *policy*—and then, new *programs* for the agency. The agency may be seen in the role of a seller. The President

18. This point is brought out in an excellent discussion of the pros and cons of the centralized and decentralized approaches appearing in OECD, *Science, Growth, and Society: A New Perspective* (Paris: OECD, 1971), pp. 65–69.

and Congress must act on behalf of the people as buyers. Unless a buyer is sophisticated and can challenge the agency or can identify what it needs, the buyer can become the victim of the seller (or, at least, *some* sellers). For, in the decentralized, *de facto* policy model, certain agencies are much better than others at planning, protecting, and marketing their programs in a politically attractive way. Certain agencies have greater intensity of interest in science and technology. Some agencies have more bureaucratic power; they have technical and tactical expertise and a strong and supportive constituency.

The consequence of these variations among agencies is great unevenness, in terms of discovery and promotion of R&D options. Important programs that the nation needs may not become part of national policy under the decentralized model, simply because of the ineptitude or political impotence of their administrative backing. Central leaders must know not only when to say "No" to a powerful seller, but also when to reach down into the agencies to help pull a laggard technology that is not getting the administrative push it needs. Some central support may be particularly essential for basic research in periods when budgets are tight and universities unpopular. Perhaps science and technology programs move all too swiftly in certain sectors where there is the necessary administrative backing. Where that help is either nonexistent or feeble, relative to institutional forces opposing innovation, programs are slow to be launched and quick to be terminated.

STRATEGIC NATIONAL POLICY

The governance of federal science and technology is not wholly decentralized. But it is obvious that this country's R&D system is closer to that pattern than the more centralized model that was implied as desirable by Lefèvre and his OECD colleagues: one guided by "a science policy, distinct from general policy, with its own aims and special administration and programmes." There is no central "ministry" for science and technology in the United States. Policy and administration are decentralized and diffused among a host of operating agencies. Nevertheless, the technoscience agencies are not entirely self-governed. Federal science and technology policy comes close to administrative laissez-faire, but there are certain central initiatives. Some derive from the constant pressure from OMB to cut programs in order to save money. The more dramatic and creative (although infrequent) central initiatives tend to be ad hoc macropolitical reactions to "crises." Both routine and "crisis-related" central initiatives provide some movement, some adjustment of the system-as-a-whole to new threats and challenges. No doubt, enterprising agencies can use a crisis for their own interests, but other agencies find themselves subjected to reorganization and new legislation. On the whole, budgeting and crisis-related decisions represent two of the more important external checks on the technoscience agencies.

Missing, however, is a capacity for initiative at the national level that starts with the questions: Where, as a nation, do we wish to go? What instruments—administrative, scientific, technological, and social—can get us there? What new tools do we wish to develop that will provide new options? Such a strategic approach does not start with the agencies and their R&D capabilities and incrementalist plans, nor from the narrow budgetary standpoint of OMB, nor from topside, reactive crisis decisions. It begins from a national perspective on intermediate and long-term problems and opportunities. It releases the future from the vested interests of the present—and the past. It permits system-wide change, with a minimum of disruption and damage to the scientific and technological institutions on which the country depends. Such a strategic national policy would be broader than R&D *per se*. In fact, it would place science and technology in their proper place, as tools of national policy rather than as instruments of administrative ambition or victims of bureaucratic inertia and self-restraint. Such an approach would be far more likely to incorporate a broad set of interests than the present decentralized, pluralistic system. Policy-making/implementation would still be decentralized. Too much centralization is as dangerous as too much administrative laissez-faire. "Mistakes" under centralized systems tend, in fact, to be bigger than those that occur in more incremental polities.[19] A *pure, strategic* national policy is probably neither possible nor desirable, but there should be more policy leadership from the political estate at the national level (as contrasted with subsystem levels). Policy-planning must take place sooner, higher up, with "general" policy utilizing specialized policy, rather than vice versa.

President Nixon talked "strategic" and acted ad hoc, or not at all. Reliance on technoscience agencies and episodic central reactions is not unrelated to the wishes of the Founding Fathers to keep national power weak, particularly to keep the Chief Executive from becoming too strong vis-à-vis Congress, the states, and the people. Incrementalist, muddling-through decision-making provides some predictability to governance, although what it predicts may not always be desirable since it tends to be more of the same.

The twin issues of governmental power and balance cannot be avoided. The dilemma is not one of power *per se,* but of democratic control of power. It is especially one of balance between power at the national level and power at the admin-

---

19. For example, under Stalin and Khrushchev, centralized research administration proved disastrous for Soviet genetics. A high-ranking agricultural scientist-administrator, Trofim Lysenko, opposed a theory of heredity accepted by most geneticists and supported the doctrine that characteristics acquired through environmental influences are inherited. Because of Lysenko's political connections, his theories were offered as Marxist orthodoxy. In 1948 they won official support of the Soviet Central Committee. Other approaches were regarded as against the interest of the State. In the early 1960's Lysenko's theories fell from power. In the meantime, however, Soviet genetics had suffered a terrible setback.

istrative level. How can general and specialized governmental institutions and policies be better integrated? In the twentieth century, executive branch authority has grown. Vast bureaucracy has come into being: "a fourth branch of government" with its most recent addition being a scientific and technological arm of remarkable potential.

The Constitution separated power, but the requirements of governmental action united power around functional administration. Congress, with its duty to authorize and appropriate funds, to investigate agencies, as well as to advise and consent on appointments of top administrative executives, has as much legal authority over administration as the President. The nature of Congress, which delegates its own power to expert committees and subcommittees, reinforces specialized administration, at the expense of general authority, to set directions for the country-as-a-whole. Congressional careers, as well as bureaucratic careers, are advanced by whatever enhances the function with which they are associated.

In other words, what the Constitution divides and weakens at the top of government tends to be filled in the middle layers by administrative/congressional alliances about specific functions. Hence, a vacuous national policy finds itself standing opposite relatively cohesive fiefdoms of sectoral policy. Some sectors are strong, some weak; but, in the aggregate, they are a significant force opposing central, general political initiative. This is the major problem facing the governance of science and technology. It goes to the issue of whether democracy, as it operates in the United States, can effectively utilize science and technology in coping with growing internal and external challenges.

There is need for more central planning to deal with problems that are clearly cross-functional and that arise from emerging difficulties which lack a strong administrative/congressional base in existing structures. That means cooperation between the *two* prime executives: the President and Congress-as-a-whole. Central science and technology advice and machinery are needed.[20] Scientific and engineering "foresight"[21] must be linked as concretely to policy-making at the top as it is to the administrative levels of government. However, the problems of governing R&D are not due to insufficient technical advice to the President and Congress. There is plenty of information available—including technical information—independent of agencies. What tends to be lacking is collective national political leadership that makes use of such information.

The political estate—particularly Congress—is heavily involved in the administration of programs. Its more important task lies in governing. Governing requires thinking *across* the agencies and *beyond* the present, in ways that represent *all* the interests of the public. That is a tall order, but that is what democratic government in the post-industrial era urgently requires. A great deal can be done to strengthen the strategic policy role of central political institutions without necessarily restructuring American government in fundamental ways. For example, the principal division of power within Congress lies between the party and the committee leadership. As committee leaders find it in their interest to unite with agencies in functional politics, the party leaders of Congress have common stakes with the President in rallying around broader national goals, if only to protect their own decision-making prerogatives.[22] The two congressional budget committees and supporting congressional budget office staff, as well as the Office of Technology Assessment, provide instruments that could be used by central congressional policy leadership. It would be extremely helpful if the legislative

20. See E. B. Skolnikoff and H. Brooks, "Science Advice in the White House? Continuation of a Debate," *Science,* Vol. 187, January 10, 1975, pp. 35–46.
21. "Foresight" was the primary contribution science advisers could bring to top political leaders, in the view of C. P. Snow. See his *Science and Government* (Cambridge: Harvard University Press, 1961), p. 81.
22. On the general subject of the bureaucracy and political leadership, see Richard E. Neustadt, "Politicians and Bureaucrats," in David B. Truman, ed., *The Congress and America's Future* (New York: Columbia University Press, 1965), pp. 102–20.

mandates of agencies could be periodically reviewed by Congress and the President with an eye to questioning whether such mandates required overhauling and updating. Such a process might have the effect of lifting administrative policy out of the subsystem mode into a broader and more inclusive arena through forcing attention to fundamental issues. Unless the capacity to make strategic policy is enhanced, the United States will have no alternative but to continue to rely primarily on administrative policy punctuated by piecemeal, reactive decisions from the center. Ad hoc national policymaking by crisis is firefighting—albeit at the macro scale.

CONCLUSION

The contribution of technoscience agencies and those interests associated with them relate to the creation, maintenance, and extension of programs along existing and specialized lines of emphasis. The inertia of agencies can sometimes have a positive value in accomplishing long-term public objectives. In contrast, the contribution of a strategic national policy ought to lie in facilitating change: starting major new programs and ending obsolete programs to which particular agencies have become wedded. Both kinds of emphases are needed. Properly balanced, strategic and administrative policy can help the country to meet threats and realize opportunities, to improve the lot of its citizens, and to play a positive role in world affairs. One should not, however, expect the technoscience agencies to fulfill the function of the national political leadership.

Science and technology have no independent minds of their own. They are instruments of people and institutions— *certain* people and institutions. This study has focused on the pivotal relationship of science and technology to large-scale, administrative agencies of the United States government. Together, science, technology, and public organization *could* constitute a new means to improve the human condition for all mankind. But that requires better direction by present political will. "The greatest invention of the nineteenth century," Alfred North Whitehead once wrote, "was the invention of the method of invention."[23] In the twentieth century, the method of invention has been harnessed to certain sectors of governmental power. By the year 2000, this vast capability may yet be made more fully the instrument of democratic purpose. That will depend upon what we do today.

23. Alfred North Whitehead, *Science and the Modern World*, Mentor Edition (New York: New American Library, 1962), p. 91.

Index